The Anti-Inflammatory Diet & Action Plans

The Anti-Inflammatory
Diet & Action Plans

4-WEEK MEAL PLANS TO HEAL THE IMMUNE SYSTEM AND RESTORE OVERALL HEALTH

DOROTHY CALIMERIS & SONDI BRUNER

SONOMA
PRESS

DOROTHY

To everyone who is cooking their way to a better and healthier life.

SONDI

To those struggling or suffering with a chronic condition:
There is hope, and it can be found on the plate.

Tips to Reduce Chronic Inflammation

CHOOSE PLENTY OF FRUITS AND VEGETABLES Our most potent warriors in the fight against inflammation are fruits and vegetables. They are packed with numerous macro- and micronutrients that support our health, including antioxidants, fiber, vitamins, minerals, and amino acids, as well as phytonutrients that possess anti-inflammatory and anti-cancer properties.

CONSUME HEALTHY SOURCES OF FAT Fat is a superhero, not a villain. Omega-3 fatty acids, found in foods like salmon, sardines, walnuts, chia seeds, flaxseed, hemp seeds, and even vegetables like dark leafy greens, are especially anti-inflammatory. These powerhouse foods also boost mood, improve cardiovascular health, balance blood sugar, enhance your immune system, and keep skin hydrated and healthy looking.

EAT ENOUGH PROTEIN Protein is essential for growth, healing, and repair of tissues, so it's crucial for managing an inflammatory condition. Too much, however, is not a good thing. Animal protein can create excess inflammation, so moderate the amount you eat; aim for vegetable sources like beans, legumes, nuts, seeds, and vegetables.

SELECT WATER AS YOUR "SIGNATURE" DRINK Water—the essential beverage—sweeps away toxins, lubricates the digestive tract, reduces pain, and minimizes allergy and asthma symptoms. Aim for at least eight glasses per day—more if you live in a warm climate or are extremely active.

MANAGE STRESS LEVELS Chronic stress impacts the body as well as the mind, suppressing our ability to regulate a proper inflammatory response, which may lead to many diseases. So take a walk, enjoy a movie, attend a yoga class, or hire a babysitter—whatever you need to feel balanced, relaxed, and supported.

CATCH PLENTY OF ZZZZS Sleep is important. It's the time when we repair, recharge, and regenerate. A poor night's sleep may lead to higher levels of inflammation, plus it leaves us vulnerable to weight gain, food cravings, moodiness, and heart disease.

Contents

Introduction

Food has always been my passion. I grew up in a home eating whole foods we often grew in our backyard. While never an athlete, I always liked to walk and my career as a chef keeps me on my feet and moving all day long. About 10 years ago I noticed that, after times of increased stress, it took longer and longer for me to bounce back. What used to take three weeks of focused eating and exercise now took three months! No matter what I did, I felt like I was riding a bike uphill.

I contacted my doctor who, in turn, diagnosed me with irritable bowel syndrome (IBS). I read all I could about it, but what I learned didn't mesh with what I was experiencing. I went to an acupuncturist. We had a long talk about my liver and gallbladder and she gave me a lot of herbs to try; they helped, but didn't manage all the symptoms. Finally, I went to a naturopathic physician, who performed comprehensive tests on my digestive tract and also blood tests to check thyroid function. The results were enlightening.

My issues were due to inflammation and food sensitivities. After completing an elimination diet, my sensitivities became very clear. My digestion issues improved, my sleep improved, and my energy returned. Armed with this information I can now make better, purposeful choices about what I eat and how to balance foods.

My lifelong passion for food allowed me to craft recipes, meals, and action plans to create healthy and delicious food minimizing and eliminating the consequences of inflammation. I share this with you here. *The Anti-Inflammatory Diet & Action Plans* provides clear direction to embrace anti-inflammatory eating. The meal plans are varied; you choose based on your unique needs and preferences. Most recipes are straightforward and can be adapted easily based on the action plan you follow.

SONDI'S STORY

It's one thing to possess knowledge, but an entirely different beast to transform that knowledge into action. When I was diagnosed with Crohn's disease at 18, I gathered all the data like the good little nerd I was: the symptoms, studies, complications, medications, treatments, and diagnostic tests.

The one thing I didn't do was learn how to eat. My doctors told me that diet didn't matter; it wouldn't help my symptoms or change the course of my disease. Since I was a teenager and felt invincible anyway, I believed that.

I was a picky eater as a child and favored foods like bread, rice, cheese, muffins, cookies, candy, and chocolate. Since my diagnosis didn't change what I ate, I continued to consume fluffy bagels and ice cream with abandon. As the years went by, my medications grew stronger yet I got sicker, bouncing in and out of the emergency room. At 23, I underwent surgery to remove a foot of small bowel—and I still didn't consider changing my diet or lifestyle. Why would I, when no one thought there was a correlation between my diet and my disease?

By my mid-20s I was perpetually swollen with painful bloating and could barely keep my eyes open. My gastroenterologist said, "Well, you look fine"—after which I promptly hurried to a naturopathic doctor for a second opinion. She completely changed my diet, and I finally began to understand the power of food.

Following an anti-inflammatory diet has been a game-changer for me—and the elimination of gluten and dairy has been especially transformative. I'm able to manage and control my symptoms by what I choose to eat and I'm eternally grateful for that choice.

The anti-inflammatory action plans and recipes in this book offer the tools I wish I'd had all those years ago. You'll learn not only how to eat to support your health, but also discover delicious new recipes so you won't feel the least bit deprived. Supported by these tools, you'll be able to take swift and positive actions that will propel you toward better health.

Your
Action
Plans

1

Understanding Chronic Inflammation

What exactly is *inflammation*? If you've ever had a cold, a cut, a rash, or a bruise, then you've experienced inflammation. In urgent situations, inflammation is incredibly useful—similar to when emergency personnel are dispatched to help accident victims. It activates our immune system, destroys pathogens, and delivers needed oxygen and nutrients to affected areas. However, if inflammation becomes chronic, or one's immune system fails to work properly, a person can develop a host of diseases that can impact all aspects of day-to-day existence.

Inflammation—which is a growing problem worldwide—can be caused by such things as poor nutrition, environmental toxins, genetics, reliance on medication, stress, and limited physical activity. However, when educated and prepared, you can take control of your health, both preventing inflammation from happening or managing it when it occurs.

A Widespread Problem

Inflammation is a normal, healthy response to an injury or infection. It's a protective measure, designed to sweep out harmful invaders so we can repair and heal. Without inflammation, a simple cut from slicing vegetables or a bruise from banging your elbow could become quite dangerous.

Acute inflammation is short-lived, allowing us to repair and move on with our lives. *Chronic* inflammation occurs when we are unable to quash the original injury, the irritant continues to enter the body, or, as is the case with autoimmune diseases, the body begins to attack healthy tissues.

Inflammation is at the root of many diseases and conditions. Any condition that ends with "itis" involves inflammation: arthritis, colitis, endocarditis, bronchitis, appendicitis, laryngitis, just to name a few. Everyone is susceptible to inflammation, though people with weakened immune systems—children, the elderly, those with autoimmune conditions—can be at an increased risk.

Health conditions linked to inflammation include:

- *Inflammatory Bowel Disease (IBD).* This includes Crohn's disease and colitis, which occur when the digestive tract becomes inflamed, leading to poor digestion and absorption of nutrients. According to the Centers for Disease Control and Prevention (CDC) and Crohn's and Colitis Canada, more than 1 million people in the United States have IBD, and one in 150 Canadians live with the disease—the highest of any country in the world.

- *Heart Disease.* This is a broad term for a wide range of conditions that impact the cardiovascular system. The Centers for Disease Control and Prevention (CDC) report that heart disease is the leading cause of death in the United States for both men and women, killing 610,000 people every year.

- **Obesity.** Excess weight is a worldwide problem. According to the World Health Organization (WHO), obesity rates have doubled since 1980, and 1.9 billion people around the world are obese.

- **Rheumatoid Arthritis and Osteoarthritis.** Rheumatoid arthritis occurs when the body attacks its own tissues, causing inflammation in the joints. Osteoarthritis also involves inflammation, but its cause is wear and tear in the joints over time. In the United States, 52.5 million people suffer from arthritis and CDC experts predict this number will grow to 67 million by 2030.

- **Allergies.** Food, drugs, animals, plants, mold, latex, or other toxins can cause the immune system to overreact, leading to a host of uncomfortable symptoms. The American College of Allergy, Asthma & Immunology estimates that more than 50 million Americans suffer from allergies.

- **Asthma.** This disease of the lungs involves coughing, shortness of breath, and chest tightness. The National Heart, Lung, and Blood Institute says that 25 million adults and seven million children live with this condition.

- **Lupus.** This autoimmune disease involves the body attacking its own tissues, leading to inflammation in many parts of the body. The Lupus Foundation of America indicates it mostly affects young women, and about 1.5 million people in the United States have forms of lupus; a 2002 CDC report noted that African American women are three times more likely to get lupus than women of other ethnicities.

- **Hashimoto's Disease.** This is an autoimmune disease in which the immune system attacks and damages the thyroid, which can lead to swelling of the thyroid (called a goiter), among other symptoms. The journal *Thyroid Research* reports that Hashimoto's is the most common hypothyroid condition in the United States.

SHOULD I SEE A DOCTOR?

When symptoms plague you and limit your lifestyle or exercise, it's time to confirm what's happening in your body.

Write down your symptoms and the time of day they occur. Keep a food diary for a few days to help assess whether nutrition plays a role in your condition.

Describe your symptoms to your family doctor. The blood tests or procedures recommended will depend on the condition your doctor suspects, but there are two tests you can request that show general markers of inflammation.

C-Reactive Protein (CRP) This protein is produced by the liver in response to inflammation. CRP is an indication of a wide range of inflammatory conditions, including heart disease, arthritis, inflammatory bowel disease, lupus, cancer, and more.

Cortisol A hormone produced by the adrenal glands, cortisol is highly anti-inflammatory. Elevated levels may indicate inflammation.

WHAT TYPE OF PRACTITIONER SHOULD I SEE?

There are several types of health and wellness practitioners that can offer help and advice for an inflammatory condition.

Naturopathic Doctor Naturopaths combine traditional and natural forms of medicine to identify health problems at their root. Naturopaths are typically able to spend more time with patients, and may be covered by some health benefit plans.

Acupuncturist Acupuncture is a traditional Chinese therapy in which practitioners place tiny needles (don't worry, they won't hurt) at specific points of the body. A study from the *Archives of Internal Medicine* reports that acupuncture is scientifically proven to help manage chronic pain.

Nutritionist Good and informed dietary choices are crucial when dealing with inflammation. A nutritionist can design a customized, anti-inflammatory menu plan to improve your symptoms and soothe pain.

Yoga Teacher Stress management and exercise are important to managing inflammation. Yoga's deep breathing and gentle movements can help you relax, and will help reduce chronic pain, muscle tension, blood pressure, anxiety, and depression. So get your "om" on!

Mental Health Counselor Chronic diseases can be both physically and emotionally debilitating. Talking to a qualified, objective professional can reduce your emotional anxiety and help you feel supported.

- *Diabetes.* This occurs when the body doesn't produce enough insulin, or can't effectively use the insulin it creates. Many complications from diabetes involve inflammation, such as obesity, atherosclerosis, and foot ulcers. In the United States, 20.9 million people have been diagnosed with type 2 diabetes—a number that has tripled since 1980, according to the CDC.

- *Cancer.* This happens when abnormal cells grow, invade different parts of the body, and hijack healthy cells. It is the leading cause of death worldwide. According to the World Health Organization (WHO), 14 million cancer cases are diagnosed each year and that number is expected to rise by a whopping 70 percent in the next two decades.

- *Celiac Disease.* Having this autoimmune disease means the body can't process gluten, leading to damage in the small intestine. According to the National Foundation for Celiac Awareness, approximately one in 133 Americans have celiac disease, though many people go undiagnosed. Untreated celiac disease can lead to other conditions like diabetes and dermatitis herpetiformis, an uncomfortable skin condition.

- *Multiple Sclerosis (MS).* This autoimmune disease of the nervous system results in the protective coatings on nerve cells—called myelin sheaths—being attacked and damaged. This can cause vision problems, disrupted motor function, dizziness, and muscle weakness. The National Multiple Sclerosis Society estimates that 400,000 Americans suffer from MS.

- *Skin Diseases.* Inflammatory skin conditions such as eczema, acne, rosacea, and psoriasis can lead to redness, itchiness, dry skin, skin bumps, and pimples. The *Encyclopedia of Natural Medicine* says that eczema affects two to seven percent of the population, while two to four percent have psoriasis. According to the National Rosacea Society, 16 million Americans suffer from that condition.

- *Headaches.* Tension headaches usually involve a steady, dull pain or pressure, while migraines tend to have a throbbing or pounding quality. The WHO says nearly half of adults worldwide experience at least one headache a year; according to the Migraine Research Foundation, 36 million Americans are affected by migraines.

- *Brain Disorders.* Neurologist David Perlmutter, MD, author of *Grain Brain*, links inflammation and the consumption of sugar and carbs to a variety of brain disorders, including dementia, ADHD, anxiety, depression, and epilepsy.

Common Symptoms of Inflammation

There are many symptoms that may indicate inflammation in the body. In the following section, you'll discover both the obvious and not-so-obvious signs of inflammation.

Normal

Often times, inflammatory symptoms are obvious and demand your attention. They include:

- Pain and soreness
- Redness
- Swelling
- Heat

Silent

Inflammation isn't always obvious. Many people don't realize the symptoms they are experiencing are linked to inflammation. Some common signals of inflammation include:

DISEASE	POSSIBLE SYMPTOMS
Inflammatory Bowel Disease	Poor appetite, constipation, diarrhea, blood or mucus in stools, nausea, night sweats, fatigue
Heart Disease	High blood pressure, fatigue, sweating, dizziness, fluttering in the chest
Obesity	Excess weight, imbalance of blood sugar, snoring, sweating
Rheumatoid Arthritis	Fatigue, weakness, weight loss, joint stiffness
Osteoarthritis	Morning stiffness
Allergies	Food intolerances, digestive issues, acne, mental fogginess, runny nose, watery eyes, bedwetting, dizziness
Asthma	Coughing, mucus
Lupus	Fatigue, fever, hair loss, anemia, light sensitivity
Hashimoto's Disease	Weight gain, dry skin, depression, fatigue, thinning hair, cold sensitivity
Diabetes	Increased hunger, thirst, and urination
Cancer	Weight loss, fatigue, fever
Celiac Disease	Weight loss, fatigue, digestive issues, greasy stools
Multiple Sclerosis	Blurred vision, dizziness, tingling, weakness
Skin Conditions	Digestive problems, family history of allergies
Headaches	Nausea, blurred vision, dull ache
Brain Disorders	Memory loss, insulin resistance, anxiety, decreased cognitive function, behavioral changes

Lifestyle and Medical Interventions

The medical community addresses inflammation with a range of medications and lifestyle practices. It's important to know what is available and to work with your doctor to find the best treatment for you.

Some medications prescribed to treat inflammation include:

- *Nonsteroidal Anti-Inflammatory Drugs (NSAIDs).* This group of drugs blocks a specific group of enzymes, which prevents the production of inflammatory chemicals. Popular NSAIDs include aspirin and ibuprofen. Long-term use of NSAIDs can increase the risk of stomach ulcers.

- *Corticosteroids.* This group of drugs deactivates the genes activated during the inflammatory process. They are used to control a wide range of chronic conditions.

- *Acetaminophen.* This drug (often branded as Tylenol in the US and known as paracetamol in Europe) helps manage pain from chronic conditions, but it doesn't prevent or address inflammation.

Popular lifestyle practices your doctor may recommend to help with inflammation are:

- *Rest.* A good night's sleep will help reduce inflammation, heal and repair tissue, boost memory, and control appetite. Aim for at least eight hours each night, and try to put down electronic devices at least one hour before bedtime.

- **Stress management.** Whether you're experiencing work, family, or financial stress, applying stress management techniques can reduce your inflammatory load. Mediation, enjoying nature, walking, reading, deep breathing, and even sitting down for a cup of tea can help you relax and reduce stress.

- **An anti-inflammatory diet.** A nutritious diet loaded with vegetables, fruits, protein, fiber, healthy fats, antioxidants, and clean water play an enormous role in putting out the fires of inflammation.

For more specific and targeted strategies, speak with your doctor or health-care professional.

2

Empowered Eating
for Healthy Living

There are many things in life that are beyond our control, but if you're lucky, your diet is not one of them. Good nutrition plays a crucial role in the prevention, development, and management of chronic inflammatory conditions.

It's important to know about foods that worsen inflammation, the best anti-inflammatory fare to include in your diet, and how you can follow an anti-inflammatory diet whether you're following a Vegan, Paleo, or Mediterranean Action Plan.

With this information, you can make smart choices at the grocery store to fuel and enhance a healthy lifestyle.

Foods that Worsen Inflammation

Food plays an extremely important role in the inflammatory response. Food choices can either soothe inflammation, or cause it to worsen. The following section details the foods that should be avoided on an anti-inflammatory diet, as well as where they might be lurking in seemingly innocent foods.

Gluten

Gluten is a protein found in wheat, wheat germ, barley, rye, spelt, kamut, farro, bulgur, semolina, farina, and triticale. As gluten is hard to digest it can cause intestinal and digestive problems. People with celiac disease have a specific immune response to a protein in gluten called *gliadin*, where the immune cells destroy the microvilli in the small intestine, which absorb nutrients. But gluten causes more than digestive distress—it can also be responsible for brain fog, sinus problems, joint pain, blood sugar imbalances, hormonal imbalances, and skin conditions.

Despite media reports that gluten-free diets are only necessary for those with celiac disease, gluten consumption can worsen a wide range of chronic diseases. Anyone with virtually any inflammatory condition can benefit from a gluten-free diet.

The key to a healthy gluten-free diet is focusing on fresh, whole, naturally gluten-free foods. Skip the gluten-free cookies and gluten-free bagels and choose fruits, vegetables, gluten-free grains, beans, legumes, nuts, seeds, lean meat, and fish instead. A diet rich in these foods will provide the nutrients you need to thrive and leave you feeling satisfied.

GLUTEN-CONTAINING FOODS TO AVOID

Gluten is often used as a binder or thickener in foods and, as such, these food can be a hidden source of it. Read food labels carefully and know these primary sources to check for gluten:

Beer	Cookies	Pasta sauce
Bread	Croutons	Pastries
Bread crumbs	Deli meats	Salad dressings
Cakes	Flour	Sauces
Candy	Gravies	Soups
Cereal	Pasta and noodles	Soy sauce

Dairy

Children are taught that dairy is an essential food to grow big and strong. However, many people don't produce the lactase enzyme required to digest the lactose sugars in milk, leading to bloating, gas, and diarrhea. In addition to lactose intolerance, milk allergies are quite common, and are one of the top allergies in North American children as noted by both FARE—Food Allergy Research and Education—and the American College of Allergy, Asthma, and Immunology.

Milk is a mucus-forming food, and when that mucus coats the digestive tract it prevents nutrients from being absorbed. Dairy cows raised for conventional milk products are fed growth hormones and antibiotics, which can interfere with our hormones and lead to inflammation. Additionally, conventional dairy products are often loaded with sugar and preservatives (especially the low-fat ones) and this can further contribute to inflammatory processes.

While this information applies to many, it's good to note that some people may be able to eat dairy even though it's on the "foods to avoid" list. For more information on why this is the case, refer to Foods with Sensitivity Alerts (see page 40).

DAIRY FOODS TO AVOID

Butter	Cream cheese	Kefir
Cheese	Frozen yogurt	Milk and cream
Cottage cheese	Ice cream	Yogurt

Corn

Because so much corn today is genetically modified, it is a food to avoid. About 90 percent of corn in the United States is genetically engineered. Genetically modified organisms (GMOs), or genetically modified foods, are relatively new to our food system and can pose potentially serious health risks. As a result of the modifications, they can suppress the immune system and promote inflammation. Corn is ubiquitous in processed foods; for instance, high-fructose corn syrup is prevalent in the majority of processed, sugary treats. And vegetable oils like corn oil are higher in omega-6 fatty acids, which are also inflammatory.

CORN-CONTAINING FOODS TO AVOID

Corn	Corn syrup	High-fructose
Corn flour	Corn tortillas	corn syrup
Cornmeal	Dextrose	Maltodextrin
Corn oil	Dextrin	Maize
Corn starch	Golden syrup	Maltose
Corn sugar		Xanthan gum

Soy

Similar to corn, this controversial bean is a common allergen. A recent report from the US Department of Agriculture's Economic Research Service states that 93 percent of soy grown in the United States is genetically modified. Soy is high in *goitrogens*, compounds that can suppress thyroid function. Soy also contains anti-nutrients such as phytates and oxalates, which interfere with digestion and disrupt the endocrine system.

SOY FOODS TO AVOID

Bean curd	Soy isolate	Soy sauce
Edamame	Soy lecithin	Soy yogurt
Miso	Soy milk	Tamari
Soybeans	Soy nut butter	Tempeh
Soy flakes	Soy nuts	Textured vegetable
Soy flour	Soy oil	protein (TVP)
Soy ice cream	Soy protein	Tofu

Peanuts

A common allergen, peanuts contain a carcinogenic mold called *aflatoxin*, which can affect those with liver conditions or candida. Peanut crops are heavily treated with pesticides and this can lead to further inflammation or allergic reactions. They are also high in omega-6 fatty acids, a pro-inflammatory fat, and conventional peanut butters are loaded with added sugar and trans fats.

Caffeine

Can't survive without that morning caffeine jolt or afternoon pick-me-up? If you're suffering from inflammation, consider nixing your caffeine habit. Caffeine propels the stomach to release its contents prematurely, injecting undigested food into the small intestine, where it can aggravate the digestive tract. Caffeine sends blood sugar soaring, raises blood pressure and heart rate, suppresses appetite, and disrupts sleep. To put the final nail in the caffeine coffin, it stresses the nervous system, which can interfere with cortisol levels. Some practitioners recommend avoiding raw cocoa powder as well, because cocoa (and any chocolate product) contains caffeine.

Alcohol

While the occasional glass of wine offers a positive hit of anti-oxidants, excess consumption of alcohol can increase the production of C-reactive protein (CRP), a marker of inflammation.

Many alcoholic beverages are loaded with sugar, which can wreak havoc on blood sugar levels, cause headaches, and suppress the immune system. Alcohol also destroys gut flora, an integral part of the digestive system. Poor intestinal flora can lead to a leaky gut, where particles of food break through the intestinal barrier and activate the immune system, inducing further inflammation and allergies.

Citrus Foods

Most citrus foods are acidic and can provoke inflammation in people with conditions such as gastroesophageal reflux disease (GERD), arthritis, and citrus sensitivities. To buffer the acidity, the body pulls from its pool of alkaline minerals such as calcium, magnesium, and potassium. Without this buffer, the acid can place undue stress on the body, leaving one susceptible to disease.

When used in moderation, though, lemons and limes can be a handy addition to an anti-inflammatory diet as they kick-start digestion and enhance liver detoxification. Once metabolized by the body, they leave alkaline minerals behind. Some other types of citrus also contain beneficial antioxidants and anti-inflammatory nutrients, and can be helpful if consumed sparingly. Overall, however, it is better to avoid them.

CITRUS FOODS TO LIMIT OR AVOID

Clementines	Limes	Tangelos
Grapefruit	Oranges	Tangerines
Lemons	Pomelos	Satsumas

Feedlot Animal Products

Conventional animal products from large, industrial animal farms—the biggest producers of meat in the US—cause inflammation for a variety of reasons. Animals are fed hormones and antibiotics, which has caused a growing worldwide problem of antibiotic resistance. As determined by the Food and Drug Administration (FDA), and reported in *The Atlantic* (October 2014), 80 percent of all antibiotics sold in the United States are given to animals, and bacteria have begun to adapt to these drugs. This reduces the efficacy of antibiotics in humans and makes illnesses more difficult to treat.

Animals are often fed fare that is different from their natural diet. In feedlots, animals are mostly given grains like wheat and GMO corn, along with GMO soy—all of which are pro-inflammatory. Grain-fed animals also yield meat that is higher in inflammatory omega-6 fatty acids. As the old adage says, "Garbage in, garbage out." But you can avoid this dilemma.

Choose organic products from animals raised without hormones or antibiotics, with outdoor access, and fed a mix of grass and grain. If you don't have access to organic meat, check with your local farmer—sometimes farms follow organic practices, but cannot afford to become certified organic (it's very expensive to do so). Simply ask! You may find it's easier to access naturally raised meats and dairy than you thought.

FEEDLOT ANIMAL FOODS TO AVOID

Beef	Dairy	Goat
Broth	(non-organic)	Lamb
(non-organic)	Eggs	Pork
Chicken	Gelatin	Sheep
		Turkey

Sugar

There is no getting around it: White, refined sugar is harmful to health. It spikes blood sugar, which increases the production of inflammatory cytokines (the chemical messengers involved in our immune response). Sugar also produces advanced glycation end products (AGEs), substances that damage cells and play a role in aging and disease.

As if that weren't bad enough, sugar also damages teeth, robs bodies of vitamins and minerals, causes mood swings, and inhibits immune systems.

Artificial or Processed Foods

Processed foods contain many ingredients that contribute to inflammation: chemicals, preservatives, unhealthy fats, excess sugars, additives, artificial food dyes, refined carbohydrates, and synthetic vitamins and minerals the body cannot process, and more.

As a general rule, if there is an ingredient on a food label you can't make at home or you won't find in nature, the best practice is to leave the product on the shelf.

Eggs

According to Health Canada, eggs are a top allergen in North America and can be difficult to digest; many people are sensitive or intolerant to their protein. Feedlot eggs are particularly high in inflammatory nutrients, such as omega-6 fatty acids.

While this information applies to many, it's good to note that some people may be able to eat eggs even though they're on the "foods to avoid" list. For more information on why this is the case, refer to Foods with Sensitivity Alerts (see page 40).

And on the flip side, organic pastured eggs are a great source of protein, vitamin D, omega-3 fatty acids, and B vitamins—especially choline, which is essential to the nervous system.

Nightshade Vegetables

This family of vegetables includes tomatoes, white potatoes, eggplant, peppers, and tobacco. Nightshades contain alkaloids that can cause gastrointestinal upset, and may aggravate inflammation in conditions like rheumatoid arthritis and osteoarthritis, headaches, lupus, kidney disease, gout, hypertension, and cancer.

Nightshade foods may also leach calcium from bones and redistribute it to places where it shouldn't be, like joints, kidneys, and arteries.

And, again, while this information applies to many, it's good to note that some people may be able to eat vegetables in the nightshade family even though they're on the "foods to avoid" list. For more information on why this is the case, refer to Foods with Sensitivity Alerts (see page 40).

Foods Worth Embracing

The good news: After reading about which foods to avoid, it might seem there's nothing left to eat. *Not true.* There is an abundance of foods you can enjoy and the recipes in this book show you how to prepare them deliciously. You won't feel deprived in the least!

Generally speaking, vegetables and fruits are your anti-inflammatory best friends. The following foods and food groups are packed with nutrients that prevent or reduce inflammation. Eat up!

- *Allium vegetables.* Onions, garlic, leeks, shallots, scallions, ramps, and chives offer a host of benefits. Onions are a rich source of vitamin C and quercetin (which helps relieve allergy symptoms). Onions also contain *onionin A*—a molecule that targets the immune system to prevent unwanted inflammation. Garlic is no slouch either; it contains a range of sulfurous compounds that reduce inflammation throughout the body, plus it has antiviral and antibacterial properties.

- *Apple cider vinegar.* Made from fermented apples, apple cider vinegar is a good source of probiotics and can help boost stomach acid levels. Apple cider vinegar has long been used to address a wide variety of inflammatory conditions, including Crohn's disease, colitis, arthritis, diabetes, colds, and flu. Be sure to select raw, unpasteurized apple cider vinegar to maximize its health benefits.

- *Basil.* *Eugenol*, a volatile oil found in basil, inhibits the enzymes that produce inflammation (and actually affects the same enzymes targeted by NSAIDs).

- *Berries.* Blueberries, raspberries, blackberries, and strawberries are potent sources of antioxidants that combat cellular damage and inhibit the enzymes that promote inflammation. Berries are also high in fiber, which benefits the digestive tract, cardio-vascular system, and blood sugar levels.

- *Bone broth.* Bone broth, prepared with organic animal bones, simmered for at least several hours, contains the amino acids glycine, proline, and arginine. It helps support the digestive tract by bringing digestive juices to the gut, and reduces joint pain.

- *Coconut oil and extra-virgin olive oil.* Coconut oil is a healthy saturated fat that is especially high in lauric acid, which enriches brain function and the immune system. It is easily digested and used immediately by the body for energy rather than being stored as fat.

  Extra-virgin olive oil contains numerous polyphenols that reduce the chemical messengers and enzymes that lead to inflammation.

- *Dark leafy greens.* Dark leafy greens contain the antioxidant vitamins A, C, E, and K, which combat cellular damage that can contribute to inflammation. They're also great sources of anti-inflammatory omega-3 fatty acids and B vitamins, which help manage stress and nourish the nervous system.

- *Dill.* This herb helps neutralize carcinogens and is used for digestive problems like gas, indigestion, and constipation.

- *Fennel.* This sweet vegetable contains a number of anti-inflammatory phytonutrients, but it is especially high in a compound called *anethole*. It has anti-inflammatory and anti-cancer properties, and helps shut down the signaling process that triggers inflammation. Fennel also contains antioxidants and immune-boosting nutrients.

- *Fish.* Wild salmon, sardines, anchovies, mackerel, and halibut are wonderful sources of omega-3 fatty acids—the healthy fats. Salmon, in particular, is high in two omega-3s called EPA and DHA, which help produce anti-inflammatory molecules.

- *Ginger.* This root contains anti-inflammatory compounds called *gingerols*, which inhibit pro-inflammatory molecules. Ginger is used to treat a wide variety of conditions, including digestive issues, nausea, motion sickness, arthritis, headaches, colds, and flu.

- *Gluten-free grains.* Quinoa and brown rice are used throughout the anti-inflammatory recipes here, and for good reason.

  Quinoa is a complete plant-based source of protein, which means it has the same amino acids found in animal products. Sufficient protein is key to healing inflammation. It's also a rich source of magnesium, a relaxant mineral that reduces inflammation and contains vitamin E.

  Brown rice is also high in magnesium as well as selenium, which helps with detoxification and protects cells from damage.

- *Natural sweeteners.* While refined white sugars are inflammatory, there are some natural sweeteners that can be used in an anti-inflammatory diet. Raw honey is rich in healing amino acids, digestive enzymes, and antiviral constituents—helping to enhance the immune system. Maple syrup is rich in antioxidants, plus it's high in zinc—another important nutrient for the immune system. Of course, using natural sugars is completely optional. Omit them if you prefer to avoid sweeteners completely.

- *Nuts and seeds.* Walnuts, almonds, cashews, hemp seeds, chia seeds, flaxseed, and more contain a wide range of healthy fats, protein, and fiber. Walnuts, hemp seed, chia seeds, and flaxseed are particularly high in omega-3 fatty acids.

- *Pineapple.* The core and stem of this tropical fruit contains *bromelain*, which reduces inflammation and helps protein digestion.

- *Root vegetables.* Carrots, sweet potatoes, parsnips, turnips, celery root, rutabaga, and beets are anti-inflammatory and antioxidant powerhouses.

  Carrots and sweet potatoes are rich sources of vitamin A, which helps nourish the mucosal cells in the digestive tract, aids vision, boosts the immune system, and keeps skin healthy.

  Sweet potatoes contain anthocyanin pigments and beets are full of compounds called betalains, both of which reduce the production of inflammatory enzymes.

- *Sustainable, organic meat.* Lamb, chicken, and turkey are high in protein, which is essential for healing and repairing inflammation. They are also rich in B vitamins, particularly B_{12}—a key nutrient for the nervous system rarely present in plants.

- *Turmeric.* Turmeric's anti-inflammatory power stems from *curcumin*. It can help reduce inflammation associated with inflammatory bowel disease, arthritis, cystic fibrosis, and cancer.

- *Winter squashes.* Similar to root vegetables, winter squashes contain high amounts of vitamins C and A. They also contain special compounds called *cucurbitacins* that inhibit the enzymes that lead to inflammation.

FOODS TO ENJOY OR AVOID

FOOD GROUP	ENJOY WITH GUSTO	ANTI-INFLAMMATORY ALL-STARS	FOODS TO AVOID
Dark Leafy Greens	arugula, collard greens, kale, mizuna, mustard greens, romaine lettuce, spinach, Swiss chard	arugula, collard greens, kale, mizuna, mustard greens, romaine lettuce, spinach, Swiss chard	
Root Vegetables	beets, carrots, celery root, kohlrabi, parsnips, rutabaga, sweet potatoes, turnips, yams	beets, carrots, celery root, kohlrabi, parsnips, rutabaga, sweet potatoes, turnips, yams	
Winter Squashes	acorn, butternut, delicata, hubbard, kabocha, pumpkin, spaghetti	acorn, butternut, delicata, hubbard, kabocha, pumpkin, spaghetti	
Fats and Oils	avocado, Camellia oil, coconut oil, extra-virgin olive oil, flaxseed oil, ghee (if tolerated), hemp oil	avocado, Camellia oil, coconut oil, extra-virgin olive oil, flaxseed oil, ghee (if tolerated), hemp oil	corn oil, margarine, peanut oil, rapeseed oil, soybean oil, vegetable oil
Nuts and Seeds	almonds, Brazil nuts, cashews, chia seeds, flaxseed, hemp seeds, macadamia nuts, pumpkin seeds, sesame seeds, walnuts	almonds, Brazil nuts, cashews, chia seeds, flaxseed, hemp seeds, macadamia nuts, pumpkin seeds, sesame seeds, walnuts	peanuts
Grains	amaranth, brown rice, buckwheat, millet, quinoa, sorghum, teff, wild rice		barley, bulgur, corn, couscous, farina, farro, kamut, semolina, spelt, triticale, wheat

FOOD GROUP	ENJOY WITH GUSTO	ANTI-INFLAMMATORY ALL-STARS	FOODS TO AVOID
Beans and Legumes	adzuki beans, black beans, chickpeas (if tolerated), kidney beans, lentils, lima beans, navy beans, split peas		soybeans
Fruit	apples, banana, blackberries, blueberries, cherries, kiwi, lemons, mango, peaches, pineapple, strawberries	apples, bananas, blackberries, blueberries, cherries, kiwi, lemons, mango, pineapple, strawberries	Citrus fruits: clementines, grapefruit, limes, oranges, pomelos, tangelos, tangerines, satsumas
Allium Vegetables	chives, garlic, onions, scallions, shallots	chives, garlic, onions, scallions, shallots	
Cruciferous Vegetables	broccoli, Brussels sprouts, cabbage, cauliflower, kale	broccoli, Brussels sprouts, cabbage, cauliflower, kale	
Nightshade Vegetables			eggplant, peppers, tobacco, tomatoes, white potatoes
Herbs and Spices	basil, cumin, dill, fennel seeds, ginger, rosemary, turmeric	basil, cumin, dill, fennel seeds, ginger, rosemary, turmeric	
Animal and Fish Products	anchovies, chicken, halibut, lamb, mackerel, salmon, sardines, trout, turkey	anchovies, chicken, halibut, lamb, mackerel, salmon, sardines, trout, turkey	cheese, dairy, eggs, feedlot animal products, ice cream, yogurt

Foods with Sensitivity Alerts

There are a few foods in the recipes following that are on the "Foods to Avoid" list. While this might seem strange, these ingredients cause inflammatory reactions in some people, but not in others. They include:

- *Dairy.* Some recipes contain organic goat's or sheep's milk and cheese. Goat and sheep products are more similar in nutrients to human breast milk, which is why some people can tolerate them better than cow's milk. Also, ghee—clarified butter—doesn't contain milk solids, so some don't have a problem digesting it.

- *Nightshades.* This family of vegetables can contribute to inflammation, but also contains many beneficial nutrients. When used in moderation, nightshades can be part of a healthy diet, particularly when following the Mediterranean Action Plan.

- *Eggs.* While these can be allergenic, not everyone has a reaction to them. Also, the way eggs are cooked can impact the reaction—the longer an egg is exposed to heat, the more the protein is denatured and changed. This means that a soft-poached egg might be tolerated well, but a hard-boiled or scrambled egg may cause a reaction.

Depending on each individual's health status and biochemical structure, foods affect everyone differently. While we aim to offer dietary guidelines, these aren't hard-and-fast rules. We encourage you to pay attention and listen to what your body is telling you. It's helpful to keep a food diary for a week—write down everything you eat, the time you consume it, and whether you notice any physical symptoms before, during, or after eating.

If you experience a reaction to any food or food groups, then don't consume them anymore. But if you tolerate these foods, feel free to include them as a part of your healthy, unique diet.

Following an Anti-Inflammatory Diet

In summary, these are the basic guidelines to follow, no matter which anti-inflammatory diet you select:

- Choose plenty of fruits and vegetables.
- Consume healthy sources of fat.
- Watch your omega-6 to omega-3 ratio.
- Eat enough protein.
- Heal and support your gut.
- Avoid refined sugars and processed foods.
- Drink at least eight glasses of water each day.
- Manage your stress levels.
- Get plenty of sleep.

With these points in mind, it's time to learn more about each anti-inflammatory plan and pick the one that's right for you.

The Vegan Action Plan

This anti-inflammatory Vegan Action Plan is packed with fruits, vegetables, grains, beans, legumes, nuts, seeds, and oils. *No animal products of any kind are consumed*—this includes meat, fish, fowl, eggs, and dairy; many even stay clear of honey, substituting maple syrup or coconut sugar instead.

Those following the Vegan Action Plan will want to avoid glutinous grains, soy, nightshades, and processed vegan meat substitutes as these can induce inflammation.

1. *Consume plenty of fruits and vegetables.* These are the mainstay of a vegan diet and they offer copious anti-inflammatory nutrients. Consider eliminating nightshades (potatoes, tomatoes, peppers, eggplant, etc.), from the diet, as well as corn.

2. *Eat enough plant-based protein.* Some vegans are "carbotarians," eating a lot of pasta, rice, bread, and baked goods. Plant-based protein is essential to an anti-inflammatory vegan diet because it helps repair and heal tissues. Aim for complete sources of protein, such as quinoa, hemp seeds, and chia seeds, or combine proteins whenever possible (i.e., pair brown rice with beans) to consume a full slate of amino acids.

3. *Boost omega-3 intake.* Healthy sources of fat, particularly omega-3s, are very important. Most nuts and seeds, along with green vegetables and avocado, are good sources. Further boost your intake by adding ground flaxseed or chia seeds to your food, or consume omega-3 alternatives like sea vegetables.

4. *Avoid soy products.* Many vegan diets include plenty of soy, but as soy can induce inflammation it's best to skip it.

5. *Avoid processed vegan meat or dairy substitutes.* Some products attempt to simulate the taste and texture of animals foods (like vegan chicken, tuna, sausage, or cheese), but are typically filled with preservatives, additives, or artificial flavors. Nondairy milk, yogurt, and cheese are often thickened with a stabilizer called carrageenan, a compound that causes inflammation—particularly in the digestive tract. Choose whole, plant-based foods instead.

6. *Select gluten-free grains.* Opt for brown rice, quinoa, buckwheat, millet, teff, sorghum, gluten-free oats, and wild rice over glutinous wheat, spelt, kamut, barley, and other grains.

- Plant-based diets are associated with lower risks of heart disease, obesity, diabetes, and cancer.
- Many are vegan for ethical reasons, as the diet is inherently animal friendly.

POSSIBLE CHALLENGES

- Nutrient deficiencies may occur if your diet does not include a variety of foods.
- Eliminating nightshades, soy, corn, and imitation products can leave you feeling deprived.

The Mediterranean Action Plan

The Mediterranean Action Plan can greatly reduce your risk of heart disease and stroke. An anti-inflammatory Mediterranean diet is full of vegetables, fruits, beans, nuts, seeds, fish, chicken, and healthy fats, such as those from extra-virgin olive oil.

Those following an anti-inflammatory Mediterranean diet may want to *avoid* or *limit* nightshade vegetables, soy products, and red wine or alcohol.

RULES AND PRINCIPLES

1. ***Consume plenty of fruits and vegetables.*** Most fruits and vegetables are welcome staples on this diet. Be aware, though, that some recipes corresponding to this diet contain nightshade vegetables like tomatoes, peppers, and eggplant. Try them and see how you feel afterward. If you have a reaction, eliminate nightshades for two weeks and see if there is improvement.

2. ***Limit gluten-free grains.*** While a limited amount of grain is allowed in a typical Mediterranean diet, an anti-inflammatory dieter may want to reduce grain consumption further.

3. ***Eat healthy sources of fat.*** Oily fish, such as wild salmon, sardines, anchovies, and trout, are wonderful sources of omega-3s, making them a perfect fit for this plan. Aim to eat fish two to three times per week.

4. ***Skip the red wine.*** Many are drawn to a traditional Mediterranean diet because it allows one or two glasses of red wine per day. However, it's best to omit the wine, and avoid alcohol altogether, as it can aggravate inflammatory conditions.

POTENTIAL BENEFITS

- A reduced risk of heart attack or stroke.
- Animal products are allowed.

POSSIBLE CHALLENGES

- If you enjoy that glass of wine with dinner, you might feel disappointed or deprived.
- If you have trouble with nightshades, particularly tomatoes, you may not react as well to this diet.

The Paleo Action Plan

Paleo followers consume red meat, wild game, poultry, eggs, nuts, seeds, fish, vegetables, and fruits. However, since we know that excess consumption of animal products can lead to inflammation (particularly if it comes from feedlots), this anti-inflammatory plan includes less meat.

1. *Consume fewer animal products, particularly red meat.* Traditional Paleo plans include large quantities of meat, including beef, lamb, chicken, eggs, and fish. This anti-inflammatory menu reduces the consumption of red meat and chooses more fish and poultry. Instead of eating animal products at virtually every meal, try to consume more vegetarian meals.

2. *Buy organic, pasture-raised animal products.* Animals raised on hormones, antibiotics, and GMO grains can increase inflammation levels; additionally, the meat from these animals contains higher amounts of omega-6 fatty acids. Organic, pasture-raised meat is richer in anti-inflammatory omega-3 fats.

3. *Eat plenty of fruits and vegetables.* Most vegetables and fruits are allowed on this meal plan. That said, it is recommended that you eliminate nightshade vegetables (potatoes, tomatoes, peppers, eggplant, etc.).

4. *Be mindful of egg consumption.* The traditional Paleo plan includes plenty of eggs. However, if you are intolerant, eliminate them.

5. *Include gluten-free pseudograins.* Quinoa, amaranth, and buckwheat are often referred to as grains because of the way they are cooked and used, but they are actually not grains at all—they are seeds. They are gluten-free and rich in nutrients, such as amino acids. Consuming these pseudograins can be beneficial to anti-inflammatory Paleo followers who are trying to eat less meat.

POTENTIAL BENEFITS

- Increased consumption of plant-based foods, most of which are naturally anti-inflammatory.

- Improvement in symptoms if dealing with an inflammatory condition and, perhaps, even eliminating or reducing medication.

COPING WITH CRAVINGS

An anti-inflammatory meal plan may be challenging for anyone used to refined carbohydrates, sugar, and processed foods. For the first weeks, you may feel as if your symptoms are getting worse. As your body detoxifies, it releases toxins that can cause fatigue, rashes, sinus problems, insomnia, aches, acne, moodiness, or headaches. It's called the Jarisch-Herxheimer Reaction, or a healing crisis—and it *will* pass.

Food cravings are to be expected as well. Use the following tips to cope with them:

Ask yourself, "Am I hungry?" Are you actually hungry, or are you bored, thirsty, angry, sad, depressed, frustrated, or emotional? Take a moment to think. Answering honestly will help you decide if you need food or something else.

Replace rituals. If a certain time of day or certain activities trigger food cravings, replace the eating ritual with something else. Try taking 10 deep breaths, walk around the block, enjoy a cup of tea or a glass of water, or have a good stretch.

Eat mindfully. Don't eat while driving, working, watching TV, or standing at the kitchen counter. Put food on a plate and pay attention to each bite, noticing how your food looks, tastes, and smells. Mom was right: chew your food well— this helps digestion immensely.

Discover healthier versions of the foods you crave. Depriving yourself of foods you love will only lead to binging (and guilt). Make homemade versions of your favorite guilty pleasures or swap candy for fresh or dried fruit, exchange potato chips for baked or dehydrated kale chips, or substitute salty snacks with salted nuts or trail mix.

Balance your blood sugar. Consume adequate amounts of protein, healthy fats, complex carbohydrates, and fiber during each meal or snack. This ensures you stay satiated and balances blood sugar levels.

Uncover nutrient deficiencies. People often crave sugar or carbs when protein-deficient, crave chocolate when they need magnesium, reach for French fries when they need a healthy fat, and dive into salty snacks if they require minerals. Recognize what you truly need and find a healthy alternative.

- Consuming a lot of organic, grass-fed animal products, along with nuts and seeds, can be expensive.

- Difficulty finding high-quality sources of animal products.

- A grain-free and nightshade-free diet can feel restrictive and limited.

The Time-Saving Action Plan

This plan is perfect if you want to save time in the kitchen while benefitting from an anti-inflammatory diet, but don't want to follow a strict dietary philosophy like veganism, Mediterranean, or Paleo. This plan allows a wider array of foods to eat—as long as you don't have any known food allergies or intolerances. The meals on this plan will keep you fueled and healthy.

The recipes for the Time-Saving Plan are quick and easy to prepare—they take 15 minutes or less, with the exception of slow cooker recipes. These involve about 15 minutes of prep work, after which you can leave everything in the slow cooker and forget about it. Healthy, anti-inflammatory eating has never been so simple or delicious!

POTENTIAL BENEFITS

- Less time in the kitchen prepping and cooking, while still reaping the benefits of an anti-inflammatory diet. Plus, the quick prep and cooking times may lead to some stress reduction.

- A wider variety of foods is available, so you feel less restricted.

POSSIBLE CHALLENGES

- Symptoms may persist if you are still consuming foods that don't agree with you (i.e., grains, meat, nightshades, or eggs).

3

Anti-Inflammatory Action Plans

Menu planning is the number one nutritional tool you can use to support your health. The best intentions to eat well won't matter if you don't have a strategy in place to help you reach your goals.

Following a menu plan has many benefits—you take control of your well-being, dine in a way that moderates inflammation, and reduce your risk of disease. On a day-to-day basis, you'll feel empowered, less stressed, and even excited at the prospect of the delicious meals you prepare at home.

Menu plans teach organizational, culinary, and budgeting skills that are invaluable to a healthy diet. Once you learn how to eat in a way that works best for your body, you'll *feel* healthy, vibrant, and energetic. Can a menu plan do all that? Absolutely!

Making the Anti-Inflammatory Action Plans Work for You

There are four wonderful, anti-inflammatory menu plans to choose from:

1. **VEGAN**
2. PALEO
3. MEDITERRANEAN
4. **TIME-SAVING**

Each 28-day Action Plan includes suggestions for breakfast, lunch, dinner, and snacks. Each uses affordable, easy-to-find ingredients, and the recipes require only about 30 minutes of active preparation time (except for the Time-Saving Plan, where each recipe takes no more than 15 minutes). Some recipes include substitution suggestions and sensitivity alerts for problematic ingredients.

To set yourself up for success, follow these handy tips to make the plans work for you.

1. *Schedule time each week to grocery shop.* Menu planning won't happen if you don't make it a priority. Dedicate a specific day and time each week to purchase and prepare ingredients for your plan. Do this on a less busy day to help reduce stress.

2. *Prep ingredients immediately.* Wash and chop ingredients in bulk for recipes in the upcoming week. Slice vegetables, juice a few lemons, and cut meat into cubes. The time it takes to fix many meals is mostly spent prepping, not cooking.

3. *Cook in advance.* To relieve the pressure of cooking during the busy week, prepare some dishes in advance. For instance, you could make dinner for the first two days of the plan, cook an enormous batch of brown rice to use throughout the week, or place ingredients for your morning smoothie in a jar and leave it in the freezer, ready to blend the next day.

4. ***Enlist family or friends for help.*** Don't do everything alone. Ask family, friends, or roommates to help with the prepping or cooking. This completes the job faster and makes it more enjoyable. Get the kids involved, too, teaching them valuable skills that will set them up for success later in life.

5. ***Make it fun and pleasurable.*** Prepping and cooking doesn't have to be boring. Turn on your favorite tunes, listen to a podcast, catch up on TV shows, or chat with a friend on speakerphone. Enjoy a non-food reward each week when the prepping is complete—like settling down with a good book you've been meaning to read or taking a walk on a beautiful day.

6. ***Batch-cook favorite recipes.*** As you move through the plans, you'll undoubtedly discover dishes you love. Double, or even triple, those recipes. Freeze extra portions for later. Your healthy self with thank you. Likewise, dinner leftovers make great lunches, and a large batch of grains one day can be reheated for breakfast the next.

7. ***Keep simple options on hand.*** Celery and carrots with hummus or nut butter, avocados, nuts, seeds, jicama sticks, and berries are all fast and easy snacks to keep on hand. Make double batches of Mini Snack Muffins (page 126) or Buckwheat Waffles (page 104) and freeze in single servings for quick heat-and-eats throughout the week.

8. ***Don't give up.*** If you're not used to cooking, it may seem daunting, tedious, or difficult at first. Cooking improves with practice. As the weeks pass, you'll get into a groove and become faster and more efficient. As your symptoms improve, you'll feel more energetic and motivated to continue, as well.

Each Action Plan is anti-inflammatory, immune boosting, digestive supporting, and delicious. So, which to choose? Read on for each plan's overview to help you decide.

The **VEGAN** *Action Plan*

A diet high in plant-based protein, complex carbohydrates, fiber, and healthy fats, this Action Plan is great for vegetarians or vegans. If you want to increase your plant consumption and explore plant-based recipes, this is a great way to start. However, for anyone who cannot tolerate beans, legumes, or grains, this is not the plan for you. Likewise, meat lovers be forewarned: you may not be fully satisfied.

WEEK

1

MONDAY

Breakfast: Inflammation-Soothing Smoothie (page 80)

Lunch: Fennel, Leek, and Pear Soup (page 132)

Dinner: Mushroom Risotto (page 175)

TUESDAY

Breakfast: Coconut Rice with Berries (page 97)

Lunch: Brussels Sprout Slaw (page 151)

Dinner: Quinoa-Broccolini Sauté (page 168)

WEDNESDAY

Breakfast: Eat-Your-Vegetables Smoothie (page 81)

Lunch: Fennel, Leek, and Pear Soup (leftovers)

Dinner: Hummus Burgers (page 185), with sliced tomatoes and cucumbers

THURSDAY

Breakfast: Overnight Muesli (page 99)

Lunch: Mushroom Risotto (leftovers)

Dinner: Lentil, Vegetable, and Fruit Bowl (page 161)

FRIDAY

Breakfast: Protein Powerhouse Smoothie (page 88)

Lunch: Sweet Potato and Rice Soup (page 139)

Dinner: One-Pot Tomato Basil Pasta (page 180)

SATURDAY

Breakfast: Mushroom "Frittata" (page 109), with melon wedges

Lunch: One-Pot Tomato Basil Pasta (leftovers)

Dinner: Savory Zucchini Patties (page 183), with Sliced Apple, Beet, and Celery Salad (page 148)

SUNDAY

Breakfast: Buckwheat Waffles (page 104)

Lunch: Sliced Apple, Beet, and Celery Salad (leftovers) with White Bean Dip (page 115), and vegetable sticks

Dinner: Butternut Squash and Spinach Gratin with Lentils (page 176)

SUGGESTED SNACKS

Celery and ¼ cup of almond butter

Fruit and 8 ounces plain nondairy yogurt

Jicama and mango wedges

Half an avocado sprinkled with sea salt

Apple and ½ cup of almonds

Chocolate-Avocado Mousse with Sea Salt (page 243)

Crunchy-Spicy Chickpeas (page 123)

MONDAY

Breakfast: Chai Smoothie (page 89)

Lunch: Mushroom "Frittata" (leftovers)

Dinner: Soba Noodle Soup with Spinach (page 137)

TUESDAY

Breakfast: Buckwheat Waffles (leftovers)

Lunch: Savory Zucchini Patties (leftovers)

Dinner: Butternut Squash and Spinach Gratin with Lentils (leftovers)

WEDNESDAY

Breakfast: Chia Breakfast Pudding (page 96)

Lunch: Hummus Burgers (leftovers), with half an avocado with sea salt

Dinner: Coconut Curry–Butternut Squash Soup (page 136)

THURSDAY

Breakfast: Green Apple Smoothie (page 84)

Lunch: Soba Noodle Soup with Spinach (leftovers)

Dinner: Buddha Bowl (page 173)

WEEK

2

FRIDAY

Breakfast: Spicy Quinoa (page 100)

Lunch: Coconut Curry–Butternut Squash Soup (leftovers)

Dinner: Zucchini Stuffed with White Beans and Olives (page 178)

SATURDAY

Breakfast: Buckwheat Crêpes with Berries (page 101)

Lunch: Avocado and Mango Salad (page 149)

Dinner: Broccoli and Lentil Stew (page 140)

SUNDAY

Breakfast: Sweet Potato Hash (page 111)

Lunch: Roasted Vegetable Soup (page 130)

Dinner: Mediterranean Chopped Salad (page 154)

SUGGESTED SNACKS

Chocolate-Avocado Mousse with Sea Salt (page 243)

Crunchy-Spicy Chickpeas (page 123)

Jicama and mango wedges

Celery with ¼ cup of almond butter

Mashed Avocado with Jicama Slices (page 116)

Chocolate-Cherry Clusters (page 248)

Chia Breakfast Pudding (page 96)

WEEK

3

MONDAY

Breakfast: Buckwheat Crêpes with Berries (leftovers)

Lunch: Zucchini Stuffed with White Beans and Olives (leftovers)

Dinner: Roasted Vegetable Soup (leftovers)

TUESDAY

Breakfast: Protein Powerhouse Smoothie (page 88)

Lunch: Broccoli and Lentil Stew (page 140)

Dinner: Buckwheat Noodle Pad Thai (page 177)

WEDNESDAY

Breakfast: Buckwheat Waffles (leftovers)

Lunch: Quinoa and Roasted Asparagus Salad (page 155)

Dinner: Winter Squash and Kasha Stew (page 141)

THURSDAY

Breakfast: One-for-All Smoothie (page 85)

Lunch: Almost Caesar Salad (page 150)

Dinner: Mango and Black Bean Stew (page 144)

FRIDAY

Breakfast: Overnight Muesli
(page 99)

Lunch: Veggie Soft Tacos
(page 184)

Dinner: Buckwheat Noodle
Pad Thai (leftovers)

SATURDAY

Breakfast: Buckwheat Waffles
(page 104)

Lunch: Winter Squash and
Kasha Stew (leftovers)

Dinner: Roasted Broccoli and
Cashews (page 170)

SUNDAY

Breakfast: Mushroom "Frittata"
(page 109)

Lunch: Quinoa-Broccolini Sauté
(page 168)

Dinner: Mediterranean Chopped
Salad (page 154)

SUGGESTED SNACKS

Half an avocado with sea salt

Celery and ¼ cup of almond butter

Pear and ½ cup of almonds

Carrot sticks and ¼ cup of hummus

*¼ cup Green Olive Tapenade
(page 260), with cucumber slices*

*Chocolate-Avocado Mousse
with Sea Salt (page 243)*

Blueberry Crisp (page 239)

MONDAY

Breakfast: Coconut Rice
with Berries (page 97)

Lunch: Mediterranean
Chopped Salad (leftovers)

Dinner: Roasted Sweet Potatoes
and Pineapple (page 165)

TUESDAY

Breakfast: Inflammation-Soothing
Smoothie (page 80)

Lunch: Mushroom "Frittata"
(leftovers)

Dinner: Lentil and Carrot Soup
with Ginger (page 135)

WEDNESDAY

Breakfast: Buckwheat Waffles
(leftovers)

Lunch: Brussels Sprout Slaw
(page 151)

Dinner: Buddha Bowl (page 173)

THURSDAY

Breakfast: Green Apple Smoothie
(page 84)

Lunch: Roasted Sweet Potatoes
and Pineapple (leftovers)

Dinner: Roasted Cauliflower
with Almond Sauce (page 162)

WEEK

4

FRIDAY

Breakfast: Overnight Muesli
(page 99)

Lunch: Lentil and Carrot Soup
with Ginger (leftovers)

Dinner: Mushroom Risotto
(page 175)

SATURDAY

Breakfast: Spicy Quinoa
(page 100)

Lunch: Roasted Vegetable Soup
(page 130)

Dinner: Butternut Squash and
Spinach Gratin with Lentils
(page 176)

SUNDAY

Breakfast: Buckwheat Crêpes
with Berries (page 101)

Lunch: Butternut Squash and
Spinach Grain with Lentils
(leftovers)

Dinner: Mushrooms in Broth
(page 131), and Green Beans
with Crispy Shallots (page 164)

SUGGESTED SNACKS

Half an avocado with sea salt

Jicama and mango wedges

Celery and ¼ cup of hummus

*Endive leaves with ¼ cup of
Green Olive Tapenade (page 260)*

*Chocolate-Avocado Mousse
with Sea Salt (page 243)*

Blueberry Crisp (page 239)

Mini Snack Muffins (page 126)

The PALEO Action Plan

This is a high-protein, healthy fat, fiber, and low-carbohydrate diet good for those who enjoy meat and eggs. If you don't tolerate some animal products well, or if you love grains, this Action Plan may not be your cup of tea. And because the animal products should be organic and pasture raised, it can be expensive on a restrictive budget.

MONDAY

Breakfast: Inflammation-Soothing Smoothie (page 80)

Lunch: Roasted Vegetable Soup (page 130)

Dinner: Chicken Breast with Cherry Sauce (page 213)

TUESDAY

Breakfast: Chia Breakfast Pudding (page 96)

Lunch: Almost Caesar Salad (page 150)

Dinner: Salmon Baked with Leeks and Fennel (page 205)

WEDNESDAY

Breakfast: Green Apple Smoothie (page 84)

Lunch: Mediterranean Chopped Salad (page 154)

Dinner: Trout with Sweet-and-Sour Chard (page 189)

THURSDAY

Breakfast: Herb Scramble with Sautéed Cherry Tomatoes (page 108)

Lunch: Brussels Sprout Slaw (page 151)

Dinner: Sesame, Broccoli, Carrot, and Chicken Stir-Fry (page 215)

FRIDAY

Breakfast: Eat-Your-Vegetables
Smoothie (page 81)

Lunch: Pumpkin Soup with
Fried Sage (page 134)

Dinner: Coconut Chicken (page 226)

SATURDAY

Breakfast: Cucumber and Smoked-
Salmon Lettuce Wraps (page 110)

Lunch: Turmeric Chicken Salad
(page 160)

Dinner: Garlic-Mustard Lamb Chops
(page 229)

SUNDAY

Breakfast: Easy Turkey Breakfast
Sausage (page 228)

Lunch: Pumpkin Soup with
Fried Sage (leftovers)

Dinner: Sea Bass Baked with
Tomatoes, Olives, and Capers (page 193)

SUGGESTED SNACKS

Half an avocado with sea salt

Apple with 2 tablespoons of almond butter

Pear with ½ cup of hazelnuts

*Mashed Avocado with Jicama Slices
(page 116)*

Celery with ¼ cup of almond butter

Mini Snack Muffins (page 126)

Chocolate-Cherry Clusters (page 248)

WEEK

2

MONDAY

Breakfast: Chai Smoothie (page 89)

Lunch: Fennel, Leek, and Pear Soup
(page 132)

Dinner: Coconut Chicken (leftovers)

TUESDAY

Breakfast: Easy Turkey Breakfast
Sausage (page 228)

Lunch: Mediterranean Chopped Salad
(page 154)

Dinner: Coconut Curry–Butternut
Squash Soup (page 136)

WEDNESDAY

Breakfast: One-for-All Smoothie
(page 85)

Lunch: Fennel, Leek, and Pear Soup
(leftovers)

Dinner: Salmon with Basil Gremolata
(page 196)

THURSDAY

Breakfast: Chia Breakfast Pudding
(page 96)

Lunch: Almost Caesar Salad (page 150)

Dinner: Spice-Rubbed Chicken (page 222)

FRIDAY

Breakfast: Protein Powerhouse Smoothie (page 88)

Lunch: Coconut Curry–Butternut Squash Soup (page 136)

Dinner: Chicken Skewers with Mint Sauce (page 218)

SATURDAY

Breakfast: Herb Scramble with Sautéed Cherry Tomatoes (page 108)

Lunch: Chicken Lettuce Wraps (page 212)

Dinner: Mediterranean Fish Stew (page 204)

SUNDAY

Breakfast: Coconut Pancakes (page 105)

Lunch: Chicken Thighs with Sweet Potatoes (page 223)

Dinner: Mediterranean Fish Stew (leftovers)

SUGGESTED SNACKS

Celery with ¼ cup of almond butter

5 olives and cucumber slices

Apple with ½ cup of almonds

1 ounce bittersweet chocolate with ½ cup of hazelnuts

1 ounce sliced turkey with jicama sticks

Chicken Fingers with Honey-Mustard-Sesame Sauce (page 227)

Smoked Trout and Mango Wraps (page 119)

MONDAY

Breakfast: Eat-Your-Vegetables Smoothie (page 81)

Lunch: Chicken Thighs with Sweet Potatoes (leftovers)

Dinner: Sole with Vegetables in Foil Packets (page 194)

TUESDAY

Breakfast: Herb Scramble with Sautéed Cherry Tomatoes (page 108)

Lunch: Almost Caesar Salad (page 150)

Dinner: Lamb Stew (page 232)

WEDNESDAY

Breakfast: Green Apple Smoothie (page 84)

Lunch: Turmeric Chicken Salad (page 160)

Dinner: Swordfish with Pineapple and Cilantro (page 198)

THURSDAY

Breakfast: Cucumber and Smoked-Salmon Lettuce Wraps (page 110)

Lunch: Lamb Stew (leftovers)

Dinner: Mediterranean Chopped Salad (page 154)

WEEK

3

FRIDAY

Breakfast: Chai Smoothie (page 89)

Lunch: Roasted Vegetable Soup
(page 130)

Dinner: Salmon Cakes with
Mango Salsa (page 209)

SATURDAY

Breakfast: Easy Turkey Breakfast
Sausage (page 228)

Lunch: Sliced Apple, Beet, and
Celery Salad (page 148)

Dinner: Sesame-Tuna Skewers
(page 203)

SUNDAY

Breakfast: Sweet Potato Hash (page 111)

Lunch: Braised Bok Choy with Shiitake
Mushrooms (page 169)

Dinner: Garlic-Mustard Lamb Chops
(page 229)

SUGGESTED SNACKS

1 ounce smoked salmon and cucumber slices

*Chicken Fingers with Honey-
Mustard-Sesame Sauce (leftovers)*

Jicama and mango wedges

Apple with 2 tablespoons of almond butter

5 olives with cucumber slices

Celery with 2 tablespoons of almond butter

Mini Snack Muffins (page 126)

WEEK
4

MONDAY

Breakfast: Protein Powerhouse
Smoothie (page 88)

Lunch: Mushrooms in Broth (page 131)

Dinner: Chicken Thighs with
Sweet Potatoes (page 223)

TUESDAY

Breakfast: Sweet Potato Hash
(leftovers)

Lunch: Turmeric Chicken Salad
(page 160)

Dinner: Oven-Roasted Cod with
Mushrooms (page 199)

WEDNESDAY

Breakfast: Inflammation-Soothing
Smoothie (page 80)

Lunch: Chicken Thighs with
Sweet Potatoes (leftovers)

Dinner: Baked Spice Salmon Steaks
(page 206)

THURSDAY

Breakfast: Easy Turkey Breakfast
Sausage (leftovers)

Lunch: Coconut Curry–Butternut
Squash Soup (page 136)

Dinner: Salmon Baked with Leeks
and Fennel (page 205)

FRIDAY

Breakfast: One-for-All Smoothie
  (page 85)

Lunch: Chicken Lettuce Wrap
  (page 212)

Dinner: Lamb Stew (page 232)

SATURDAY

Breakfast: Coconut Pancakes
  (page 105)

Lunch: Spice-Rubbed Chicken
  (page 222)

Dinner: Coconut Curry–Butternut
  Squash Soup (leftovers)

SUNDAY

Breakfast: Herb Scramble with
  Sautéed Cherry Tomatoes (page 108)

Lunch: Spice-Rubbed Chicken
  (leftovers)

Dinner: Pecan-Crusted Trout
  (page 192)

SUGGESTED SNACKS

Half an avocado with sea salt

Celery with 1/4 cup of almond butter

Pear with 1/2 cup of hazelnuts

*1 ounce smoked salmon with
  cucumber slices*

*Mashed Avocado with Jicama Slices
  (page 116)*

*Smoked Trout and Mango Wraps
  (page 119)*

Mini Snack Muffins (leftovers)

The MEDITERRANEAN *Action Plan*

Don't be fooled into thinking an anti-inflammatory Mediterranean diet is full of pasta, wine, and cheese—it definitely is not. This Action Plan is for anyone who thoroughly enjoys plant-based foods, but likewise enjoys the occasional animal product. It's high in protein, fiber, and heathy fat, and low in carbohydrates. If Mediterranean flavors aren't your favorite, this plan is probably not for you. Try the Vegan, Paleo, or Time-Saving Plans instead.

WEEK

1

MONDAY

Breakfast: Inflammation-Soothing Smoothie (page 80)

Lunch: Almost Caesar Salad (page 150)

Dinner: Salmon Baked with Leeks and Fennel (page 205)

TUESDAY

Breakfast: Herb Scramble with Sautéed Cherry Tomatoes (page 108)

Lunch: Salmon Baked with Leeks and Fennel (leftovers)

Dinner: Chicken Chili with Beans (page 142)

WEDNESDAY

Breakfast: Eat-Your-Vegetables Smoothie (page 81)

Lunch: Turmeric Chicken Salad (page 160)

Dinner: Trout with Sweet-and-Sour Chard (page 189)

THURSDAY

Breakfast: Chia Breakfast Pudding (page 96)

Lunch: Chicken Chili with Beans (leftovers)

Dinner: One-Pot Tomato Basil Pasta (page 180)

FRIDAY

Breakfast: Protein Powerhouse
Smoothie (page 88)

Lunch: Lentil, Vegetable, and
Fruit Bowl (page 161)

Dinner: Mushroom Risotto
(page 175)

SATURDAY

Breakfast: Buckwheat Waffles
(page 104)

Lunch: One-Pot Tomato Basil
Pasta (leftovers)

Dinner: Chicken Thighs with
Sweet Potatoes (page 223)

SUNDAY

Breakfast: Coconut Pancakes
(page 105)

Lunch: Chicken Skewers with
Mint Sauce (page 218)

Dinner: Garlic-Mustard
Lamb Chops (page 229)

SUGGESTED SNACKS

5 olives and cucumbers

Half an avocado with sea salt

Pear and ½ cup of walnuts

Celery and ¼ cup of hummus

Bunch of grapes and ½ cup of almonds

Chocolate-Cherry Clusters (page 248)

Mini Snack Muffins (page 126)

MONDAY

Breakfast: Chai Smoothie (page 89)

Lunch: Quinoa and Roasted
Asparagus Salad (page 155)

Dinner: Oven-Roasted Cod with
Mushrooms (page 199)

TUESDAY

Breakfast: Buckwheat Waffles
(leftovers)

Lunch: Chicken Thighs with Sweet
Potatoes (leftovers)

Dinner: Whitefish with Spice Rub
(page 191)

WEDNESDAY

Breakfast: Green Apple Smoothie
(page 84)

Lunch: Fennel, Leek, and Pear Soup
(page 132)

Dinner: Hummus Burgers
(page 185), with sliced cucumbers,
tomatoes, and avocado

THURSDAY

Breakfast: Chia Breakfast
Pudding (page 96)

Lunch: Buckwheat Noodle
Pad Thai (page 177)

Dinner: Spice-Rubbed Chicken
(page 222)

WEEK
2

FRIDAY

Breakfast: One-for-All Smoothie
(page 85)

Lunch: Lentil and Carrot Soup
with Ginger (page 135)

Dinner: Sesame, Broccoli, Carrot,
and Chicken Stir-Fry (page 215)

SATURDAY

Breakfast: Mushroom "Frittata"
(page 109)

Lunch: Fennel, Leek, and
Pear Soup (leftovers)

Dinner: Savory Zucchini
Patties (page 183)

SUNDAY

Breakfast: Buckwheat Crêpes with
Berries (page 101), and goat cheese

Lunch: Lentil, Vegetable, and
Fruit Bowl (page 161)

Dinner: Lamb Stew (page 232)

SUGGESTED SNACKS

*Cucumber slices with 1 ounce of sheep's
milk feta cheese*

Apple with 2 tablespoons of almond butter

Celery with ¼ cup of hummus

*1 ounce bittersweet chocolate with
½ cup of hazelnuts*

*Smoked Turkey–Wrapped Zucchini
Sticks (page 122)*

Chocolate-Cherry Clusters (page 248)

Mini Snack Muffins (page 126)

WEEK

3

MONDAY

Breakfast: Inflammation-Soothing
Smoothie (page 80)

Lunch: Lamb Stew (leftovers)

Dinner: Savory Zucchini Patties
(leftovers)

TUESDAY

Breakfast: Mushroom "Frittata"
(leftovers)

Lunch: Hummus Burgers
(leftovers)

Dinner: Mediterranean
Fish Stew (page 204)

WEDNESDAY

Breakfast: Chai Smoothie (page 89)

Lunch: Turmeric Chicken Salad
(page 160)

Dinner: Cod with Lentils and
Vegetables (page 200)

THURSDAY

Breakfast: Buckwheat Crêpes with
Berries (leftovers), and goat cheese

Lunch: Cod with Lentils and
Vegetables (leftovers)

Dinner: Mushroom Risotto
(page 175)

FRIDAY

Breakfast: Protein Powerhouse
  Smoothie (page 88)

Lunch: Mediterranean Chopped
  Salad (page 154)

Dinner: Lentil-Lamb Ragu
  (page 233)

SATURDAY

Breakfast: Spicy Quinoa (page 100)

Lunch: Mushroom Risotto (leftovers)

Dinner: Salmon Cakes with Mango Salsa
  (page 209)

SUNDAY

Breakfast: Sweet Potato Hash (page 111)

Lunch: Lentil-Lamb Ragu (leftovers)

Dinner: Sesame-Tuna Skewers (page 203)

SUGGESTED SNACKS

Celery and ¼ cup of hummus

*Sliced cucumbers and tomatoes with
  extra-virgin olive oil and sea salt*

Half an avocado with sea salt

*5 olives and 1 ounce of sheep's milk
  feta cheese*

Apple and 2 tablespoons of almond butter

*Celery with ¼ cup of Green Olive
  Tapenade (page 260)*

Chocolate-Cherry Clusters (page 248)

MONDAY

Breakfast: Green Apple Smoothie
  (page 84)

Lunch: Salmon Cakes with Mango Salsa
  (leftovers)

Dinner: Chicken Breast with
  Cherry Sauce (page 213)

TUESDAY

Breakfast: Sweet Potato Hash (leftovers)

Lunch: Soba Noodle Soup with Spinach
  (page 137)

Dinner: Pecan-Crusted Trout (page 192)

WEDNESDAY

Breakfast: Chai Smoothie (page 89)

Lunch: Almost Caesar Salad (page 150)

Dinner: Chicken with Brown Rice and
  Snow Peas (page 217)

THURSDAY

Breakfast: Overnight Muesli (page 99)

Lunch: Winter Squash and Kasha Stew
  (page 141)

Dinner: Sea Bass Baked with Tomatoes,
  Olives, and Capers (page 193)

WEEK

4

FRIDAY

Breakfast: One-for-All
Smoothie (page 85)

Lunch: Soba Noodle Soup with
Spinach (leftovers)

Dinner: Coconut Chicken (page 226)

SATURDAY

Breakfast: Coconut Pancakes
(page 105)

Lunch: Winter Squash and
Kasha Stew (leftovers)

Dinner: Salmon with Basil
Gremolata (page 196)

SUNDAY

Breakfast: Herb Scramble with
Sautéed Cherry Tomatoes (page 108)

Lunch: Coconut Chicken (leftovers)

Dinner: Chicken with Fennel and
Zucchini (page 214)

SUGGESTED SNACKS

Half an avocado with sea salt

*Celery and ½ cup of Green Olive
Tapenade (page 260)*

Apple with 2 tablespoons of almond butter

*5 olives and 1 ounce of sheep's milk
feta cheese*

*1 ounce bittersweet chocolate and
¼ cup of hazelnuts*

Chocolate-Cherry Clusters (page 248)

Crunchy-Spicy Chickpeas (page 123)

The TIME-SAVING *Action Plan*

Variety is the spice of life, and this high-protein, high-fiber Action Plan, with moderate amounts of healthy fats and carbohydrates, offers plenty of it. It's also the ideal plan for anyone who doesn't want to spend a lot of time preparing meals—just 15 minutes or less.

However, there are a number of recipes in this plan that use ingredients that may be problematic for anyone with multiple food allergies or sensitivities. Scan the recipes thoroughly before deciding on this plan, or substitute other recipes if you don't mind a bit more prep time.

MONDAY

Breakfast: Inflammation-Soothing Smoothie (page 80)

Lunch: Coconut Curry–Butternut Squash Soup (page 136)

Dinner: Chicken Chili with Beans (page 142)

TUESDAY

Breakfast: Warm Chia-Berry Nondairy Yogurt (page 102)

Lunch: Mediterranean Chopped Salad (page 154)

Dinner: Chicken with Brown Rice and Snow Peas (page 217)

WEDNESDAY

Breakfast: Eat-Your-Vegetables Smoothie (page 81)

Lunch: Coconut Curry–Butternut Squash Soup (leftovers)

Dinner: Lamb Stew (page 232)

THURSDAY

Breakfast: Overnight Muesli (page 99)

Lunch: Chicken Chili with Beans (leftovers)

Dinner: Avocado and Mango Salad (page 149)

WEEK

1

FRIDAY

Breakfast: One-for-All
Smoothie (page 85)

Lunch: White Bean and Tuna Salad
(page 156)

Dinner: Lamb Stew (leftovers)

SATURDAY

Breakfast: Cucumber and
Smoked-Salmon Lettuce Wraps
(page 110)

Lunch: Almost Caesar Salad
(page 150)

Dinner: Lentil-Lamb Ragu
(page 233)

SUNDAY

Breakfast: Protein Powerhouse
Smoothie (page 88)

Lunch: White Bean and Tuna Salad
(leftovers)

Dinner: Coconut Chicken
(page 226)

SUGGESTED SNACKS

Celery with 2 tablespoons of almond butter

Fruit and 8 ounces plain nondairy yogurt

Jicama and mango wedges

Half an avocado with sea salt

Apple and ½ cup of almonds

*Chocolate-Avocado Mousse with
Sea Salt (page 243)*

Chocolate-Cherry Clusters (page 248)

WEEK

2

MONDAY

Breakfast: Green Apple Smoothie
(page 48)

Lunch: Avocado and Mango Salad
(page 149)

Dinner: Coconut Chicken (leftovers)

TUESDAY

Breakfast: Spicy Quinoa (page 100)

Lunch: Coconut Curry–Butternut
Squash Soup (page 136)

Dinner: White Bean and Tuna Salad
(page 156)

WEDNESDAY

Breakfast: Chai Smoothie (page 89)

Lunch: Coconut Curry–Butternut
Squash Soup (leftovers)

Dinner: One-Pot Tomato Basil
Pasta (page 180)

THURSDAY

Breakfast: Herb Scramble with
Sautéed Cherry Tomatoes (page 108)

Lunch: Brussels Sprout Slaw (page 151)

Dinner: One-Pot Tomato Basil
Pasta (leftovers)

FRIDAY

Breakfast: Inflammation-Soothing Smoothie (page 80)

Lunch: White Bean and Tuna Salad (leftovers)

Dinner: Mediterranean Chopped Salad (page 154)

SATURDAY

Breakfast: Chia Breakfast Pudding (page 96)

Lunch: Sliced Apple, Beet, and Celery Salad (page 148)

Dinner: Winter Squash and Kasha Stew (page 141)

SUNDAY

Breakfast: Eat-Your-Vegetables Smoothie (page 81)

Lunch: Almost Caesar Salad (page 150)

Dinner: Chicken Chili with Beans (page 142)

SUGGESTED SNACKS

5 olives and cucumber slices

Carrot sticks with ¼ cup of hummus

Jicama and mango wedges

Fruit and 8 ounces plain nondairy yogurt

1 ounce smoked salmon and cucumbers

Chocolate-Avocado Mousse with Sea Salt (page 243)

Chocolate-Cherry Clusters (page 248)

WEEK

3

MONDAY

Breakfast: One-for-All Smoothie (page 85)

Lunch: Winter Squash and Kasha Stew (leftovers)

Dinner: One-Pot Tomato Basil Pasta (page 180)

TUESDAY

Breakfast: Warm Chia-Berry Nondairy Yogurt (page 102)

Lunch: Chicken Chili with Beans (leftovers)

Dinner: One-Pot Tomato Basil Pasta (leftovers)

WEDNESDAY

Breakfast: Protein Powerhouse Smoothie (page 88)

Lunch: Sliced Apple, Beet, and Celery Salad (page 148)

Dinner: Coconut Chicken (page 226)

THURSDAY

Breakfast: Overnight Muesli (page 99)

Lunch: Coconut Chicken (leftovers)

Dinner: Mediterranean Chopped Salad (page 154)

FRIDAY

Breakfast: Green Apple Smoothie
  (page 84)

Lunch: Avocado and Mango Salad
  (page 149)

Dinner: White Bean and Tuna Salad
  (page 156)

SATURDAY

Breakfast: Cucumber and
  Smoked-Salmon Lettuce Wraps
  (page 110)

Lunch: White Bean and Tuna Salad
  (leftovers)

Dinner: Lamb Stew (page 232)

SUNDAY

Breakfast: Chai Smoothie (page 89)

Lunch: Lamb Stew (leftovers)

Dinner: Mediterranean Chopped Salad
  (page 154)

SUGGESTED SNACKS

Carrot Sticks with ¼ cup of hummus

Pear with ½ cup of hazelnuts

*1 ounce smoked salmon with
  cucumber slices*

Celery with 2 tablespoons of almond butter

Half an avocado with sea salt

*1 ounce bittersweet chocolate with ½ cup
  of hazelnuts*

Kale Pesto (page 261), with vegetables

WEEK 4

MONDAY

Breakfast: Inflammation-Soothing
  Smoothie (page 80)

Lunch: Brussels Sprout Slaw
  (page 151)

Dinner: Winter Squash and
  Kasha Stew (page 141)

TUESDAY

Breakfast: Chia Breakfast Pudding
  (page 96)

Lunch: Mediterranean Chopped Salad
  (page 154)

Dinner: Winter Squash and
  Kasha Stew (leftovers)

WEDNESDAY

Breakfast: Eat-Your-Vegetables
  Smoothie (page 81)

Lunch: Almost Caesar Salad (page 150)

Dinner: Chicken Curry (page 225)

THURSDAY

Breakfast: Spicy Quinoa (page 100)

Lunch: Almost Caesar Salad (page 150)

Dinner: Chicken Chili with Beans
  (page 142)

FRIDAY

Breakfast: Protein Powerhouse
Smoothie (page 88)

Lunch: Chicken Chili with Beans
(leftovers)

Dinner: Brussels Sprout Slaw
(page 151)

SATURDAY

Breakfast: Herb Scramble with
Sautéed Cherry Tomatoes
(page 108)

Lunch: Chicken with Brown Rice
and Snow Peas (page 217)

Dinner: White Bean and Tuna Salad
(page 156)

SUNDAY

Breakfast: Chai Smoothie
(page 89)

Lunch: Avocado and Mango Salad
(page 149)

Dinner: Chicken with Brown Rice
and Snow Peas (leftovers)

SUGGESTED SNACKS

*Cucumber-Yogurt Dip (page 114),
with vegetables*

Celery with ¼ cup of almond butter

Carrot sticks with ¼ cup of hummus

5 olives with cucumber slices

Apple with 2 tablespoons of almond butter

*1 ounce bittersweet chocolate with
½ cup of hazelnuts*

Jicama and mango wedges

Kitchen Equipment and Pantry Lists

The best way to succeed with your anti-inflammatory Action Plan is to create an environment for success. Get rid of foods that cause inflammation; you may crave them in the early stages, but if they are not readily available, you're less likely to indulge. Stock your pantry with staples that help you prepare delicious, healing meals.

As with any meal plan, bland does not have to be on the menu. There are myriad herbs, spices, oils, sweeteners, and a variety of condiments that can be used to keep your meals flavorful and satisfying. Here are some tasty suggestions to get yourself on the road to better health.

DRIED HERBS AND SPICES

Cardamom, ground
Chipotle powder
Cinnamon, ground
Coriander, ground
Cumin, ground
Curry powder
Garlic powder

Ginger, ground
Mustard powder
Nutmeg, ground
Onion powder
Oregano
Peppercorns,
  black and white

Rosemary
Sage
Sea salt
Sumac
Turmeric

GLUTEN-FREE FLOURS

Almond meal or flour
Coconut flour
Brown rice or
  white rice flour

CANNED AND JARRED FOODS

Chicken broth, low-sodium
Coconut milk, full-fat
Vegetable broth

OIL, VINEGAR, AND CONDIMENTS

Aminos, coconut

Mustard, Dijon
(no added sugar)

Oil, coconut

Oil, extra-virgin olive

Vinegar, apple cider

Vinegar, balsamic

NONDAIRY MILK

Almond milk, unsweetened

Coconut milk, unsweetened

Rice milk, unsweetened

SWEETENERS

Honey, raw

Maple syrup

OTHER ITEMS

Baking powder

Baking soda

Vanilla extract

SUBSTITUTIONS TO ACCOMMODATE FOOD ALLERGENS

The recipes in this book are easily adaptable to address any food allergies, sensitivities, or intolerances. Pay attention to what your body tells you about a specific food, as eating it can lead to irritation and inflammation. Here are some simple swaps you can implement as you prepare meals:

Instead of eggs: Mix 1 tablespoon ground flaxseed or chia seeds with 4 tablespoons warm water. Stir, and let the mixture thicken for a few minutes.

Instead of tree nuts: Swap seeds such as sunflower, pumpkin, flaxseed, hemp, or chia. In most cases, you'll be able to swap these in a 1:1 ratio. You'll get a similar crunchy texture as you would from tree nuts.

Instead of shellfish: Opt for salmon, herring, trout, halibut, anchovies, sardines, or mackerel.

Essential Equipment

In addition to a well-stocked pantry, you'll want to have the right equipment to prepare your meals. The good news is these recipes can be prepared with equipment you likely have and use regularly; no specialized equipment is needed. Anything you don't have is available for affordable prices and will be a great investment as you'll use it again and again to prepare delicious anti-inflammatory meals.

Good Knives

A good knife makes all the difference when preparing meals. It's great to have a chef's knife, a paring knife, and a serrated knife on hand. The best knife to buy is the knife that fits you. Pick up the knife and feel the weight; notice how the length of the blade works for you. The right knife should feel good in your hand and be easy to manipulate. It's worth it to purchase a sharpener, or to make a commitment to regularly get your knives professionally sharpened. Always keep your fingers tucked in when chopping.

Pots and Pans

You can do little wrong with a large cast-iron pan. Once seasoned, it requires very little oil to cook with, and browns food beautifully. For recipes that start on the stove and finish in the oven, a cast-iron pan is one-stop shopping. You can often find deals on vintage cast-iron cookware at tag sales on eBay—look for brands like Wagner or Griswold. Even old, rusty pans can be resurrected with some steel wool and elbow grease, followed by a a good seasoning. Don't be afraid to find a bargain. These pans last forever. There may even be some in a family member's basement, just waiting to come back to life. In addition, a large, nonstick large skillet is helpful for making recipes like Buckwheat Crêpes (page 101). When shopping for non-stick pans, look for ceramic ones; avoid traditional nonstick pans, as there is some evidence that the chemical coating can flake into food. Finally, an omelet pan is great for rounding out your collection.

Many of the recipes in this book call for a Dutch oven or large pot with a lid. These are versatile vessels because they go from stove to oven. They can be used for long, slow braises and stews in the oven, as well as to make soups on the stove. The best are enameled cast iron.

Slow Cooker

A slow cooker is a true time-saver; for instance, you can prepare your ingredients before work, throw them in your slow cooker, and dinner is waiting when you get home. Or fill it with steel-cut oats or other grains before bedtime and wake up to a hearty breakfast. The size of the slow cooker you purchase should correspond with the volume of food you cook regularly. Make sure it has low, medium, and high settings, or a high setting with a four- and six-hour option, and a low setting with an eight- and twelve-hour option. A slow cooker is also perfect for doubling or tripling recipes and freezing the extras.

Food Processors and Blenders

A food processor is indispensable for puréeing, slicing, chopping, and shredding. For smoothies, a blender is the best tool for pulverizing fruits, vegetables, and ice.

Now that you're armed with anti-inflammatory information, determined your best Action Plan, stocked your pantry, and gathered your equipment, it's time to get cooking.

2

The Recipes

4

Smoothies & Drinks

Inflammation-Soothing Smoothie

SERVES 1 / PREP TIME: 10 MINUTES

• VEGAN

• PALEO

• MEDITERRANEAN

• TIME-SAVING

NUTRITION TIP: If you want to add protein and healthy fats to this smoothie, consider adding hemp seeds or your preferred nut butter.

___

PER SERVING

Calories: 147; Total Fat: 1g; Total Carbohydrates: 37g; Sugar: 6g; Fiber: 9g; Protein: 4g; Sodium: 89mg

Prepare to be soothed. Pears are low on the glycemic index, and fennel aids digestion. Add the micronutrients of spinach and you have a vibrant antioxidant blend to start your day right. Some vegan yogurt or one-quarter of an avocado can be added for a creamy texture.

1 pear, cored and quartered
½ fennel bulb
1 thin slice fresh ginger
1 cup packed spinach
½ cucumber, peeled if wax-coated or not organic
½ cup water
Ice (optional)

In a blender, combine the pear, fennel, ginger, spinach, cucumber, water, and ice (if using). Blend until smooth.

Eat-Your-Vegetables Smoothie

SERVES 1 / PREP TIME: 10 MINUTES

This handy "go-to" smoothie peps you up when your energy is lagging. If nightshades are okay on your diet, add one small Roma tomato to the ingredients for an extra burst of nutrition.

1 carrot, trimmed

1 small beet, scrubbed and quartered

1 celery stalk

½ cup fresh raspberries

1 cup coconut water

1 teaspoon balsamic vinegar

Ice (optional)

In a blender, combine the carrot, beet, celery, raspberries, coconut water, balsamic vinegar, and ice (if using). Blend until smooth.

- VEGAN
- PALEO
- MEDITERRANEAN
- TIME-SAVING

NUTRITION TIP:
Consider adding chia seeds for a boost of protein and fiber, or goji berries for additional essential amino acids and fiber.

PER SERVING
Calories: 140; Total Fat: 1g; Total Carbohydrates: 24g; Sugar: 23g; Fiber: 8g; Protein: 3g; Sodium: 293mg

Cherry Smoothie

SERVES 1 / PREP TIME: 10 MINUTES

- VEGAN
- PALEO
- MEDITERRANEAN
- TIME-SAVING

VEGAN TIP: If you're following the Vegan Action Plan, use the maple syrup instead of the honey.

PER SERVING
Calories: 266; Total Fat: 2g; Total Carbohydrates: 52g; Sugar: 48g; Fiber: 6g; Protein: 3g; Sodium: 122mg

Cherries—loaded with antioxidants—are known for their ability to soothe joint pain. They are combined here with raspberries, which are high in vitamin C, and coconut water, which contains electrolytes. Freeze these as ice pops for a healthy, cheery, cherry snack.

1 cup frozen no-added-sugar pitted cherries
¼ cup fresh, or frozen, raspberries
¾ cup coconut water
1 tablespoon raw honey or maple syrup

1 teaspoon chia seeds
1 teaspoon hemp seeds
Drop vanilla extract
Ice (optional)

In a blender, combine the cherries, raspberries, coconut water, honey, chia seeds, hemp seeds, vanilla, and ice (if using). Blend until smooth.

Green Apple Smoothie

SERVES 1 / PREP TIME: 10 MINUTES

- VEGAN
- PALEO
- MEDITERRANEAN
- TIME-SAVING

NUTRITION TIP:
A nondairy protein powder will provide additional protein and minerals.

VEGAN TIP: If you're following the Vegan Action Plan, use the maple syrup in place of the honey.

PER SERVING
Calories: 176; Total Fat: 1g; Total Carbohydrates: 41g; Sugar: 34g; Fiber: 6g; Protein: 2g; Sodium: 110mg

In addition to providing that apple a day, this smoothie contains coconut water, apples, lemon, and spinach—ingredients that all alkalize your system. This smoothie is particularly good when you've indulged a bit too much. To increase its stomach-soothing capabilities add a thick slice of fennel.

½ cup coconut water

1 green apple, cored, seeded, and quartered

1 cup spinach

¼ lemon, seeded

½ cucumber, peeled and seeded

2 teaspoons raw honey, or maple syrup

Ice (optional)

In a blender, combine the coconut water, apple, spinach, lemon, cucumber, honey, and ice (if using). Blend until smooth.

One-for-All Smoothie

SERVES 1 / PREP TIME: 10 MINUTES

This fruity, creamy drink is a good way to get your family to eat—and truly enjoy—their fruits and vegetables. Feel free to replace the berries with local, seasonal fruits, and to use almond milk instead of coconut milk for a low-fat option.

1 cup packed spinach
½ cup fresh blueberries
½ banana

1 cup coconut milk
½ teaspoon vanilla extract

In a blender, combine the spinach, blueberries, banana, coconut milk, and vanilla. Blend until smooth.

- VEGAN
- PALEO
- MEDITERRANEAN
- TIME-SAVING

NUTRITION TIP: Cacao nibs will add extra magnesium and be a treat for all. Just remember this will also add a jolt of caffeine.

PER SERVING
Calories: 152; Total Fat: 5g; Total Carbohydrates: 27g; Sugar: 15g; Fiber: 5g; Protein: 2g; Sodium: 90mg

Mango-Thyme Smoothie

SERVES 1 / PREP TIME: 10 MINUTES

This smoothie, neither sweet nor savory, gets some sweetness from the mango, which is balanced by the tartness of the grapes and the savory flavors of fennel, which also aids digestion, and thyme, which helps the respiratory system. The tropical-inspired blend is like a breath of fresh air to your diet, and the pepper gives it just a little kick.

- VEGAN
- PALEO
- MEDITERRANEAN
- TIME-SAVING

PER SERVING
Calories: 274; Total Fat: 4g;
Total Carbohydrates: 65g;
Sugar: 54g; Fiber: 7g;
Protein: 3g; Sodium: 125mg

1 cup fresh or frozen
  mango chunks

½ cup fresh seedless
  green grapes

¼ fennel bulb

½ cup unsweetened
  almond milk

½ teaspoon fresh
  thyme leaves

Pinch sea salt

Pinch freshly ground
  black pepper

Ice (optional)

In a blender, combine the mango, grapes, fennel, almond milk, thyme leaves, sea salt, pepper, and ice (if using). Blend until smooth.

Protein Powerhouse Smoothie

SERVES 1 / PREP TIME: 10 MINUTES

- VEGAN
- PALEO
- MEDITERRANEAN
- TIME-SAVING

NUTRITION TIP: Throw in some flaxseed for additional healthy fats, fiber, and magnesium.

PER SERVING

Calories: 500; Total Fat: 32g; Total Carbohydrates: 47g; Sugar: 34g; Fiber: 7g; Protein: 13g; Sodium: 199mg

This glass of creamy, protein-packed deliciousness delivers the nutrition you need to face the day. Avocado, hemp seed, and cashews add protein without the use of protein powder. Coconut milk and avocado provide the creamy texture. Hello day!

1 cup packed kale leaves, thoroughly washed

¼ avocado

1 cup fresh grapes

¼ cup cashews (optional)

1 tablespoon hemp seed

1 or 2 mint leaves

1 cup coconut milk

Ice (optional)

In a blender, combine the kale, avocado, grapes, cashews (if using), hemp seed, mint leaves, coconut milk, and ice (if using). Blend until smooth.

Chai Smoothie

SERVES 1 / PREP TIME: 10 MINUTES

Naturally anti-inflammatory spices give this drink the distinctive chai flavor. With sweetness from dates and bananas, this smoothie also makes a great dessert. When bananas are almost too ripe, peel, slice, and freeze them. These frozen banana pieces are great to have on hand for smoothies when the craving hits.

1 cup unsweetened almond milk

1 date, pitted and chopped

¼ teaspoon vanilla extract

½ teaspoon chai spice blend

Pinch salt

1 banana, sliced into ¼-inch rounds

Ice cubes

In a blender, combine the almond milk, date, vanilla, chai spice blend, salt, banana, and ice. Blend until smooth.

- VEGAN
- PALEO
- MEDITERRANEAN
- TIME-SAVING

RECIPE TIP: Making your own chai spice blend is easy and offers just as much (if not more!) flavor than something you purchase. Combine 1 tablespoon *each* of cinnamon, ginger, nutmeg, cardamom, and cloves. Mix well and store in a tightly sealed jar at room temperature.

PER SERVING

Calories: 171; Total Fat: 4g; Total Carbohydrates: 35g; Sugar: 20g; Fiber: 5g; Protein: 3g; Sodium: 336mg

Peachy Mint Punch

SERVES 4 / PREP TIME: 15 MINUTES

- VEGAN
- PALEO
- MEDITERRANEAN
- TIME-SAVING

INGREDIENT TIP: If the raw honey is too solid, warm it slightly before using.

VEGAN TIP: If you're following the Vegan Action Plan, use the maple syrup instead of the honey.

PER SERVING

Calories: 81; Total Fat: 0g; Total Carbohydrates: 18g; Sugar: 14g; Fiber: 1g; Protein: 0g; Sodium: 85mg

Who needs sodas and bottled drinks when you can make a delicious, fresh, fruity punch right at home? Peaches are mashed with a touch of honey and the lemon juice makes the flavors pop. Serve over ice and garnish with fresh mint sprigs for a taste of summer in a glass.

1 (10-ounce) bag frozen no-added-sugar peach slices, thawed

3 tablespoons freshly squeezed lemon juice

3 tablespoons raw honey or maple syrup

1 tablespoon lemon zest

2 cups coconut water

2 cups sparkling water

4 fresh mint sprigs, divided

Ice

1. In a food processor, combine the peaches, lemon juice, honey, and lemon zest. Process until smooth.

2. In a large pitcher, stir together the peach purée and coconut water. Chill the mixture in the refrigerator.

3. When ready to serve, fill four large (16-ounce) glasses with ice. Add 1 mint sprig to each glass. Add about ¾ cup peach mixture to each glass and top each with sparkling water.

Coconut-Ginger Smoothie

SERVES 1 / PREP TIME: 10 MINUTES

- VEGAN
- PALEO
- MEDITERRANEAN
- TIME-SAVING

VEGAN TIP: If you're following the Vegan Action Plan, use the maple syrup instead of the honey.

PER SERVING
Calories: 238; Total Fat: 18g; Total Carbohydrates: 16g; Sugar: 14g; Fiber: 10g; Protein: 5g; Sodium: 373mg

This is a coconut lover's dream, as it has both shredded coconut and coconut milk. Avocado is added for protein, and ginger contributes healing properties. Feeling adventurous? Add a small basil leaf before blending.

½ cup coconut milk

½ cup coconut water

¼ avocado

¼ cup unsweetened coconut shreds or flakes

1 teaspoon raw honey or maple syrup

1 thin slice fresh ginger

Pinch ground cardamom (optional)

Ice (optional)

In a blender, combine the coconut milk, coconut water, avocado, coconut, honey, ginger, cardamom (if using), and ice (if using). Blend until smooth.

Super Green Smoothie

SERVES 1 / PREP TIME: 10 MINUTES

This light, refreshing drink provides a fast and easy way to boost your daily intake of greens. It uses almond milk, which has less fat than coconut milk, and the touch of lemon juice and mint makes it alkalizing and soothing.

1 cup packed spinach
½ cucumber, peeled
½ pear
¼ avocado
1 teaspoon raw honey
  or maple syrup

1 cup unsweetened
  almond milk
2 mint leaves
Pinch salt
½ lemon
Ice (optional)

In a blender, combine the spinach, cucumber, pear, avocado, honey, almond milk, mint leaves, salt, 1 or 2 squeezes of lemon juice, and the ice (if using). Blend until smooth.

- VEGAN
- PALEO
- MEDITERRANEAN
- TIME-SAVING

VEGAN TIP: If you're following the Vegan Action Plan, use the maple syrup instead of the honey.

PER SERVING
Calories: 248; Total Fat: 14g;
Total Carbohydrates: 33g;
Sugar: 14g; Fiber: 10g;
Protein: 5g; Sodium: 373mg

5

Breakfast

Chia Breakfast Pudding

SERVES 4 / PREP TIME: 10 MINUTES / REST TIME: 15 MINUTES

. . . .

- VEGAN
- PALEO
- MEDITERRANEAN
- TIME-SAVING

Sensitivity Alert

VARIATION TIP: Using coconut milk instead of almond milk will make this pudding extra creamy.

VEGAN TIP: If you're following the Vegan Action Plan, use the maple syrup instead of the honey.

PER SERVING

Calories: 272; Total Fat: 14g; Total Carbohydrates: 38g; Sugar: 25g, Fiber: 6g; Protein: 7g; Sodium: 84mg

Chia seeds are a double whammy: high in fiber and a good source of protein. When combined with liquid they thicken and soften to a tapioca-like consistency. Chia puddings are so fast and easy they can be enjoyed as a snack, dessert, or for breakfast. The cashews are a good source of minerals and added protein.

Note: If you have nut sensitivities omit the cashews and use shaved coconut for that crunchy texture.

2 cups almond milk
½ cup chia seeds
¼ cup maple syrup
  or raw honey
1 teaspoon vanilla extract

1 cup frozen no-added-sugar pitted cherries, thawed, juice reserved, divided
½ cup chopped cashews, divided

1. In a quart jar with a tight-fitting lid, combine the almond milk, chia seeds, maple syrup, and vanilla. Shake well and set aside for at least 15 minutes. (You can also do this before bed and refrigerate overnight.)

2. Divide the pudding among four bowls, and top each with ¼ cup of cherries and 2 tablespoons of cashews.

Coconut Rice *with* Berries

SERVES 4 / PREP TIME: 10 MINUTES / COOK TIME: 30 MINUTES

The creaminess from the coconut milk and sweetness from the dates combine to make this a satisfying whole-grain breakfast. Toast slivered almonds and keep them on hand to add crunch and protein to any dish.

1 cup brown basmati rice

1 cup water

1 cup coconut milk

1 teaspoon salt

2 dates, pitted and chopped

1 cup fresh blueberries, or raspberries, divided

¼ cup toasted slivered almonds, divided

½ cup shaved coconut, divided

1. In a medium saucepan over high heat, combine the basmati rice, water, coconut milk, salt, and date pieces.

2. Stir until the mixture comes to a boil. Reduce the heat to simmer and cook for 20 to 30 minutes, without stirring, or until the rice is tender.

3. Divide the rice among four bowls and top each serving with ¼ cup of blueberries, 1 tablespoon of almonds, and 2 tablespoons of coconut.

• VEGAN

Sensitivity Alert

TIME-SAVING TIP: Cook the rice the night before and reheat it in the morning to save time. Or combine the rice with the water and coconut milk, and soak overnight. This shortens the cooking time.

PER SERVING

Calories: 281; Total Fat: 8g; Total Carbohydrates: 49g; Sugar: 7g; Fiber: 5g; Protein: 6g; Sodium: 623mg

Overnight Muesli

SERVES 4 TO 6 / PREP TIME: 10 MINUTES

For a stress-free morning, a little work the night before means breakfast is ready when you wake up. The apple cider vinegar adds tartness and aids digestion, but can be omitted if you prefer. The apple juice and chopped apple add fruity sweetness.

2 cups gluten-free rolled oats

1¾ cups coconut milk

¼ cup no-added-sugar apple juice

1 tablespoon apple cider vinegar (optional)

1 apple, cored and chopped

Dash ground cinnamon

1. In a medium bowl, stir together the oats, coconut milk, apple juice, and vinegar (if using).

2. Cover and refrigerate overnight.

3. The next morning, stir in the chopped apple and season the muesli with the cinnamon.

• VEGAN

• MEDITERRANEAN

• TIME-SAVING

VARIATION TIP: The beauty of muesli is you can add whatever you have on hand. Tasty additions include fresh berries, nuts, toasted coconut, flaxseed, hemp seeds, and pumpkin seeds. Just add these when you add the chopped apple.

PER SERVING

Calories: 213; Total Fat: 4g; Total Carbohydrates: 39g; Sugar: 10g; Fiber: 6g; Protein: 6g; Sodium: 74mg

Spicy Quinoa

SERVES 4 / PREP TIME: 10 MINUTES / COOK TIME: 20 MINUTES

. . . .

- VEGAN
- MEDITERRANEAN

Sensitivity Alert

TIME-SAVING TIP: If you're following the Time-Saving Action Plan, make this dish with cooked quinoa, sold in the frozen-food section of many grocery stores.

PER SERVING
Calories: 286; Total Fat: 13g;
Total Carbohydrates: 32g;
Sugar: 1g; Fiber: 6g;
Protein: 10g; Sodium: 44mg

You'll love this spicy-berry-nutty combination. Quinoa is a gluten-free seed that is high in fiber and protein. A bitter-tasting compound covers the seeds, which can irritate some people's stomachs, so it is best to rinse the quinoa well before cooking. Hemp seed is also very high in protein, but can be omitted if it's not easily found.

1 cup quinoa, rinsed well
2 cups water
½ cup shredded coconut
¼ cup hemp seeds
2 tablespoons flaxseed
1 teaspoon ground cinnamon

1 teaspoon vanilla extract
Pinch salt
1 cup fresh berries of your choice, divided
¼ cup chopped hazelnuts

1. In a medium saucepan over high heat, combine the quinoa and water.

2. Bring to a boil, reduce the heat to a simmer, and cook for 15 to 20 minutes, or until the quinoa is cooked through (it should double or triple in bulk, similar to couscous, and be slightly translucent).

3. Stir in the coconut, hemp seeds, flaxseed, cinnamon, vanilla, and salt.

4. Divide the quinoa among four bowls and top each serving with ¼ cup of berries and 1 tablespoon of hazelnuts.

Buckwheat Crêpes *with* Berries

SERVES 4 TO 6 / PREP TIME: 15 MINUTES / COOK TIME: 5 MINUTES PER CRÊPE

Crêpes take practice, but once mastered they are easy to make and make any day special. Serve these berry-filled crêpes drizzled with maple syrup, chopped nuts, and a dollop of Coconut Cream (page 266). This crêpe batter can be used to make sweet or savory crêpes.

1 cup buckwheat flour

½ teaspoon salt

2 tablespoons coconut oil
  (1 tablespoon melted)

1 ½ cups almond milk, or water

1 egg

1 teaspoon vanilla extract

3 cups fresh berries, divided

6 tablespoons Chia Jam
  (page 263), divided

1. In a small bowl, whisk together the buckwheat flour, salt, 1 tablespoon of melted coconut oil, the almond milk, egg, and vanilla until smooth.

2. In a large (12-inch) nonstick skillet over medium-high heat, melt the remaining 1 tablespoon of coconut oil. Tilt the pan, coating it evenly with the melted oil.

3. Ladle ¼ cup of batter into the skillet. Tilt the skillet to coat it evenly with the batter.

4. Cook for 2 minutes, or until the edges begin to curl up. Using a spatula, flip the crêpe and cook for 1 minute on the second side. Transfer the crêpe to a plate.

5. Continue making crêpes with the remaining batter. You should have 4 to 6 crêpes.

6. Place 1 crêpe on a plate, top with ½ cup of berries and 1 tablespoon of Chia Jam. Fold the crêpe over the filling. Repeat with the remaining crêpes and serve.

- VEGAN
- PALEO
- MEDITERRANEAN
- TIME-SAVING

VEGAN TIP: If you're following the Vegan Action Plan, omit the egg.

MEDITERRANEAN TIP: If you're following the Mediterranean Action Plan, fill each crêpe with 1 ounce of softened goat cheese along with the berries.

ACTION PLAN TIP: If you're using this recipe as part of the Vegan or Mediterranean Action Plans, double the quantities so you have enough leftovers for later in the week.

PER SERVING

Calories: 242; Total Fat: 11g; Total Carbohydrates: 33g; Sugar: 9g; Fiber: 6g; Protein: 7g; Sodium: 371mg

Warm Chia-Berry Nondairy Yogurt

SERVES 4 / PREP TIME: 10 MINUTES / COOK TIME: 5 MINUTES

- VEGAN
- PALEO
- MEDITERRANEAN
- TIME-SAVING

PER SERVING
Calories: 246; Total Fat: 10g;
Total Carbohydrates: 35g;
Sugar: 21g; Fiber: 5g;
Protein: 5g; Sodium: 2mg

A warm fruity mixture of strawberries, raspberries, and blueberries thickened with chia seeds and served with nondairy yogurt will ensure you start your day on the right (healthy) foot. Add shredded coconut and slivered almonds, or top with your favorite gluten-free granola mix, for a satisfying crunch.

1 (10-ounce) package frozen mixed berries, thawed

2 tablespoons maple syrup

2 tablespoons freshly squeezed lemon juice

½ vanilla bean, halved lengthwise

1 tablespoon chia seeds

4 cups unsweetened almond yogurt, or coconut yogurt

1. In a medium saucepan over medium-high heat, combine the berries, maple syrup, lemon juice, and vanilla bean.

2. Bring the mixture to a boil, stirring constantly. Reduce the heat to simmer and cook for 3 minutes.

3. Remove the pan from the heat. Remove and discard the vanilla bean from the mixture. Stir in the chia seeds. Let stand for 5 to 10 minutes to let the seeds thicken.

4. Divide the fruit mixture among four bowls and top each with 1 cup of yogurt.

Buckwheat Waffles

SERVES 4 / PREP TIME: 15 MINUTES / COOK TIME: ABOUT 6 MINUTES PER WAFFLE

• MEDITERRANEAN

COOKING TIP: If you don't have a waffle iron or prefer pancakes, place a large skillet over high heat. When it is hot, reduce the heat to medium and melt 1 tablespoon of coconut oil in the pan. Pour the batter into the skillet, about ¼ cup per pancake. Cook for 2 to 3 minutes, or until the pancake is brown on the bottom and bubbles form on top. Flip and cook for about 2 minutes more.

VEGAN TIP: If you're following the Vegan Action Plan, omit the egg.

STORAGE TIP: Freeze leftover waffles and reheat in the toaster for a quick breakfast.

PER SERVING
Calories: 282; Total Fat: 4g; Total Carbohydrates: 55g; Sugar: 7g; Fiber: 6g; Protein: 9g; Sodium: 692mg

Buckwheat is not a grain; it's a plant that produces grain-like seeds. Buckwheat is rich in both manganese and magnesium—minerals that improve cardiovascular health. These waffles are delicious slathered with coconut oil and topped with Chia Jam (page 263) or crushed berries. If you're using this recipe as part of the Vegan or Mediterranean Action Plan, double the quantities so you have enough leftovers for later in the week.

1½ cups buckwheat flour
½ cup brown rice flour
2 teaspoons baking powder
1 teaspoon baking soda
½ teaspoon salt
1 egg

1 tablespoon maple syrup
2 teaspoons vanilla extract
1 cup water
1½ cups almond milk
Coconut oil, for the waffle iron

1. In a medium bowl, whisk together the buckwheat flour, rice flour, baking powder, baking soda, and salt.
2. To the dry ingredients, add the egg, maple syrup, and vanilla. Slowly whisk in the water and almond milk, whisking until the batter is completely smooth.
3. Let the batter sit for 10 minutes to thicken slightly.
4. The buckwheat may settle in the bottom of the bowl while resting, so be sure to stir well before using.
5. Heat the waffle iron and brush it with coconut oil.
6. Add the batter to the waffle iron and cook according to the manufacturer's directions.

Coconut Pancakes

SERVES 4 / PREP TIME: 10 MINUTES / COOK TIME: ABOUT 5 MINUTES PER PANCAKE

....

These gluten-free pancakes are a great alternative to traditional pancakes. As the batter sits it may become thick; add some water, or coconut or almond milk to thin the consistency. Coconut pancakes can be a bit dry, so serve them with fruit and a dollop of plain nondairy yogurt.

4 eggs

1 cup coconut or almond milk, plus additional as needed

1 tablespoon melted coconut oil, or almond butter, plus additional for greasing the pan

1 tablespoon maple syrup

1 teaspoon vanilla extract

½ cup coconut flour

1 teaspoon baking soda

½ teaspoon salt

• PALEO
• MEDITERRANEAN

STORAGE TIP: These pancakes do not freeze or reheat well; plan on eating them the same day you cook them.

_____

PER SERVING

Calories: 193; Total Fat: 11g; Total Carbohydrates: 15g; Sugar: 6g; Fiber: 6g; Protein: 9g; Sodium: 737mg

1. In a medium bowl, mix together the eggs, coconut milk, coconut oil, maple syrup, and vanilla with an electric mixer.

2. In a small bowl, stir together the coconut flour, baking soda, and salt. Add these dry ingredients to the wet ingredients and beat well, until smooth and lump free.

3. If the batter is too thick, add additional liquid to thin to the consistency of traditional pancake batter.

4. Lightly grease a large skillet with coconut oil. Place it over medium-high heat.

5. Add the batter in ½-cup scoops and cook for about 3 minutes, or until golden brown on the bottom. Flip and cook for about 2 minutes more.

6. Stack the pancakes on a plate while continuing to cook the remaining batter. This makes about 8 pancakes.

Spinach Muffins

MAKES 12 MUFFINS / PREP TIME: 15 MINUTES / COOK TIME: 15 MINUTES

Spinach in muffins? People put zucchini, carrots, pumpkin, and beets in baked goods, so why not spinach? Kids love these muffins—and they never need to know they contain vegetables. Tell them they are green for good luck.

Cooking spray

2 cups packed spinach

2 eggs

¼ cup raw honey

3 tablespoons extra-virgin olive oil

1 teaspoon vanilla extract

1 cup oat flour

1 cup almond flour

2 teaspoons baking powder

1 teaspoon baking soda

½ teaspoon salt

Pinch freshly ground black pepper

1. Preheat the oven to 350°F.

2. Line or grease 12 muffin cups with cooking spray.

3. In a food processor, combine the spinach, eggs, honey, olive oil, and vanilla. Process until smooth.

4. In a medium bowl, whisk together the oat flour, almond flour, baking powder, baking soda, salt, and pepper. Transfer the spinach mixture to the bowl and mix well.

5. Fill each muffin cup two-thirds full. Place the muffins in the preheated oven and bake for about 15 minutes, or until lightly browned and the centers feel firm to the touch.

6. Transfer the pan to a cooling rack, and let cool for 10 minutes before removing the muffins from the tin.

• MEDITERRANEAN

VEGAN TIP:
Replace the eggs with a mixture of 1 tablespoon of ground flaxseed mixed with 3 tablespoons of water for each egg.

PALEO TIP: Use only almond flour instead of the combination of almond and oat flours.

PER SERVING

Calories: 108; Total Fat: 6g; Total Carbohydrates: 12g; Sugar: 6g; Fiber: 1g; Protein: 3g; Sodium: 217mg

Herb Scramble *with* Sautéed Cherry Tomatoes

SERVES 2 / PREP TIME: 5 MINUTES / COOK TIME: 10 MINUTES

- PALEO
- MEDITERRANEAN
- TIME-SAVING

Sensitivity Alert

PER SERVING
Calories: 310; Total Fat: 26g;
Total Carbohydrates: 10g;
Sugar: 3g; Fiber: 5g;
Protein: 13g; Sodium: 131mg

Oregano, garlic, and tomatoes are classic Mediterranean flavors in this high-protein breakfast. The avocado slices add micronutrients and healthy fats. This is the perfect breakfast to get you energized for a busy day.

4 eggs

2 teaspoons chopped fresh oregano

1 tablespoon extra-virgin olive oil

1 cup cherry tomatoes, halved

½ garlic clove, sliced

½ avocado, sliced

1. In a medium bowl, beat the eggs until well combined; whisk in the oregano.

2. Place a large skillet over medium heat. Once the pan is hot, add the olive oil.

3. Pour the eggs into the skillet and use either a heat-resistant spatula or wooden spoon to scramble the eggs. Transfer the eggs to a serving dish.

4. Add the cherry tomatoes and garlic to the pan and sauté for about 2 minutes. Spoon the tomatoes over the eggs and top the dish with the avocado slices.

Mushroom "Frittata"

SERVES 6 / PREP TIME: 15 MINUTES / COOK TIME: 20 MINUTES

This frittata is not really a frittata at all; eggs are replaced with a garbanzo bean batter that provides a flavorful protein base. Enjoy this with fresh fruit for breakfast or a simple green salad for lunch or dinner.

1½ cups chickpea flour

1½ cups water

1 teaspoon salt

2 tablespoons extra-virgin olive oil

1 small red onion, diced

2 pints sliced mushrooms

1 teaspoon ground turmeric

½ teaspoon ground cumin

1 teaspoon salt

½ teaspoon freshly ground black pepper

2 tablespoons chopped fresh parsley

1. Preheat the oven to 350°F.

2. In a small bowl, slowly whisk the water into the chickpea flour; add the salt and set aside.

3. In a large cast iron or oven-safe skillet over high heat, add the olive oil. When the oil is hot, add the onion. Sauté for 3 to 5 minutes, until onion is softened and slightly translucent. Add the mushrooms and sauté for 5 minutes more. Add the turmeric, cumin, salt, and pepper, and sauté for 1 minute.

4. Pour the batter over the vegetables and sprinkle with the parsley. Place the skillet in the preheated oven and bake for 20 to 25 minutes.

5. Serve warm or at room temperature.

• VEGAN

PALEO TIP: If you're following the Paleo Action Plan, omit the chickpea batter. Beat 6 eggs until frothy. Pour the eggs over the sautéed vegetables.

MEDITERRANEAN TIP: If you're following the Mediterranean Action Plan, crumble 2 ounces of goat's milk feta cheese over the batter prior to baking.

TIME-SAVING TIP: Buy the red onions already chopped and the mushrooms pre-sliced.

ACTION PLAN TIP: If you're using this recipe as part of the Vegan or Mediterranean Action Plan, double the quantities so you have enough for leftovers for later in the week.

PER SERVING

Calories: 240; Total Fat: 8g; Total Carbohydrates: 34g; Sugar: 7g; Fiber: 10g; Protein: 11g; Sodium: 792mg

Cucumber *and* Smoked-Salmon Lettuce Wraps

SERVES 4 / PREP TIME: 10 MINUTES

- PALEO
- TIME-SAVING

MEDITERRANEAN TIP:
Add 2 tablespoons of goat cheese per wrap.

PER SERVING
Calories: 107; Total Fat: 5g;
Total Carbohydrates: 6g;
Sugar: 4g; Fiber: 1g;
Protein: 11g; Sodium: 1261mg

These wraps will add a healthy touch of elegance to any brunch or lunch table. Salmon is loaded with omega-3s and is a fast and easy high-protein alternative to eggs. English cucumbers, also known as seedless cucumbers, are more digestible and taste sweeter since they contain fewer seeds.

8 large butter lettuce leaves

½ English cucumber, sliced thin

8 ounces smoked salmon, divided

1 tablespoon chopped fresh chives

4 tablespoons Almost Caesar Salad Dressing (page 256), divided

1. On a serving dish, arrange the lettuce leaves in a single layer.

2. Evenly divide the cucumber slices among the lettuce leaves. Top each leaf with 2 ounces of smoked salmon.

3. Garnish with the chives and drizzle each wrap with 1 tablespoon of Almost Caesar Salad Dressing.

Sweet Potato Hash

SERVES 4 / PREP TIME: 15 MINUTES / COOK TIME: 15 MINUTES

....

Sweet potatoes, mushrooms, and greens provide a deliciously satisfying meal with great nutrition. Turn this recipe into a timesaver by purchasing pre-sliced onions and mushrooms; or make a double batch on the weekend to enjoy all week.

2 tablespoons coconut oil

½ onion, sliced thin

1 cup sliced mushrooms

1 garlic clove, sliced thin

2 large sweet potatoes, cooked and cut into ½-inch cubes

1 cup finely chopped Swiss chard

½ cup vegetable broth

1 teaspoon salt

¼ teaspoon freshly ground pepper

1 tablespoon chopped fresh thyme

1 tablespoon chopped fresh sage

1. In a large skillet over high heat, melt the coconut oil.

2. Add the onion, mushrooms, and garlic. Sauté for about 8 minutes, or until the onions and mushrooms are tender.

3. Add the sweet potatoes, Swiss chard, and vegetable broth. Cook for 5 minutes.

4. Stir in the salt, pepper, thyme, and sage.

• VEGAN

• PALEO

• MEDITERRANEAN

NUTRITION TIP:
Vegans can add 1 cup of cooked black beans for a protein boost. If you are following the Mediterranean or Paleo Plans, crumble Easy Turkey Breakfast Sausage (page 228) into the hash.

ACTION PLAN TIP:
If you're using this recipe as part of the Vegan, Paleo, or Time-Saving Action Plan, double the quantities so you have enough for leftovers for later in the week.

PER SERVING

Calories: 212; Total Fat: 7g;
Total Carbohydrates: 35g;
Sugar: 2g; Fiber: 6g;
Protein: 30g; Sodium: 708mg

6

Snacks

Cucumber-Yogurt Dip

SERVES 4 / PREP TIME: 15 MINUTES

- VEGAN
- PALEO
- MEDITERRANEAN
- TIME-SAVING

PER SERVING
Calories: 104; Total Fat: 9g;
Total Carbohydrates: 7g;
Sugar: 2g; Fiber: 3g;
Protein: 1g; Sodium: 636mg

This is a classic tzatziki sauce made with coconut yogurt rather than the traditional dairy yogurt. Plain, unsweetened almond milk yogurt can be used, as well. Let the dip sit for at least one hour before serving to allow the flavors to develop—it makes a big difference. Serve with fresh vegetables or gluten-free crackers, or use as a sauce with chicken or fish.

1 cucumber, peeled and shredded

1 cup plain coconut yogurt

1 garlic clove, minced

1 scallion, chopped

2 tablespoons chopped fresh dill

1 teaspoon salt

2 tablespoons freshly squeezed lemon juice

2 tablespoons extra-virgin olive oil

1. Place the shredded cucumber in a fine-mesh strainer to drain.

2. In a small bowl, stir together the yogurt, garlic, scallion, dill, salt, and lemon juice.

3. Fold in the drained cucumber and spoon into a serving bowl.

4. Just before serving, drizzle with the olive oil.

White Bean Dip

MAKES 4 TO 6 SERVINGS / PREP TIME: 15 MINUTES

Simple, fast, and delicious. What's not to love? Swap garbanzo beans for the white beans to make this more hummus-like.

1 (15-ounce) can white beans, drained and rinsed

1 garlic clove

1 tablespoon tahini, or almond butter

3 tablespoons extra-virgin olive oil

¼ cup chopped pitted green olives

1 tablespoon chopped fresh parsley

¼ teaspoon salt

2 tablespoons freshly squeezed lemon juice

- VEGAN
- MEDITERRANEAN
- TIME-SAVING

Sensitivity Alert

PER SERVING
Calories: 239; Total Fat: 14g; Total Carbohydrates: 25g; Sugar: 0g; Fiber: 6g; Protein: 9g; Sodium: 358mg

1. In a food processor, combine the white beans, garlic, and tahini. With the machine running on low, slowly add the olive oil in a thin, steady stream. If the dip is too thick, thin with some water.

2. Add the olives, parsley, and salt. Pulse to combine. Stir in the lemon juice.

3. Spoon into a serving bowl and serve with raw vegetables and gluten-free crackers.

Mashed Avocado *with* Jicama Slices

SERVES 4 / PREP TIME: 15 MINUTES

- VEGAN
- PALEO
- MEDITERRANEAN
- TIME-SAVING

INGREDIENT TIP:
Avocado turns brown quickly. Slow the oxidation process by placing plastic wrap directly on top of the dip, smoothing it so there aren't any air pockets.

PER SERVING
Calories: 270; Total Fat: 20g; Total Carbohydrates: 24g; Sugar: 4g; Fiber: 15g; Protein: 3g; Sodium: 595mg

Avocado is a very versatile addition to almost any diet. This take on guacamole pairs creamy, nutrient-rich avocado with turmeric, native to southwest India and widely known for its anti-inflammatory properties. Jicama is a great source of fiber and promotes "good" bacteria in the gut—so snack on, without the guilt.

2 ripe avocados, pitted
1 scallion, sliced
2 tablespoons chopped fresh cilantro
½ teaspoon ground turmeric
Juice of ½ lemon

1 teaspoon salt
¼ teaspoon freshly ground black pepper
1 jicama, peeled and cut into ¼-inch-thick slices

1. In a small bowl, combine the scooped-out avocado, the scallion, cilantro, turmeric, lemon juice, salt, and pepper. Mash the ingredients together until well mixed and still slightly chunky.

2. Serve with the jicama slices.

Creamy Broccoli Dip

MAKES ABOUT 2 CUPS / PREP TIME: 20 MINUTES / COOK TIME: 5 MINUTES

. . . .

- VEGAN
- PALEO
- MEDITERRANEAN

STORAGE TIP: This dip will last up to 1 week in the refrigerator stored in an airtight container.

_____

PER SERVING (¼ cup)
Calories: 82; Total Fat: 7g;
Total Carbohydrates: 7g;
Sugar: 1g; Fiber: 4g;
Protein: 1g; Sodium: 628mg

Broccoli's sweet, nutty flavor is enhanced by combining it with garlic, avocado, and green onions. In addition to eating this as a dip for snacks like Sweet Potato Chips (see page 124), dollop it on omelets or grilled meats. It makes an ordinary day special.

1 cup broccoli florets
1 garlic clove
1 scallion, coarsely chopped
¾ cup unsweetened almond yogurt, or coconut yogurt
½ avocado

1 tablespoon freshly squeezed lemon juice
1 teaspoon salt
½ teaspoon dried dill
Pinch red pepper flakes

1. Fill a medium pot with 2 inches of water, place it over medium-high heat, and insert a steamer basket.

2. Add the broccoli to the steamer basket, cover, and steam for 5 minutes, or until the broccoli turns bright green. Remove the pan from the heat and drain the broccoli.

3. In a food processor, add the garlic, scallion, yogurt, avocado, lemon juice, salt, dill, and red pepper flakes. Pulse a few times until the mixture appears coarsely chopped.

4. Add the broccoli and process until well combined; the mixture should have some texture and not be completely puréed. Serve with Sweet Potato Chips (see page 124) or sticks of fresh vegetables like carrots and celery.

Smoked Trout *and* Mango Wraps

SERVES 4 / PREP TIME: 15 MINUTES

Smoked trout has a delicate, smoky flavor that is complemented by the sweetness of the mango. You can easily turn this into a salad by shredding the lettuce leaves instead of using them as a wrap.

4 large green-leaf lettuce leaves, thick stems removed

4 ounces smoked trout, divided

1 cup chopped mango, divided

1 scallion, sliced, divided

2 tablespoons freshly squeezed lemon juice, divided

1. Place the lettuce leaves on a flat surface. Top each leaf equally with pieces of the trout and mango. Sprinkle with the scallions and drizzle with the lemon juice.

2. Wrap the lettuce leaves burrito style and place them seam-side down on a serving dish.

• PALEO
• MEDITERRANEAN
• TIME-SAVING

VEGAN TIP: Replace the smoked trout with 1 cup of cooked black beans mixed with ½ teaspoon of chipotle powder for that smoky quality.

PER SERVING

Calories: 108; Total Fat: 3g; Total Carbohydrates: 13g; Sugar: 10g; Fiber: 3g; Protein: 9g; Sodium: 52mg

Kale Chips

SERVES 4 / PREP TIME: 20 MINUTES / COOK TIME: 20 MINUTES

Although kale chips are readily available and easy to buy, when you make your own you know exactly what is in them and are assured of getting all their anti-inflammatory goodness. Eat them within 24 hours, as they will lose their crunch.

1 bunch kale, thoroughly washed and dried, ribs removed, and cut into 2-inch strips

2 tablespoons extra-virgin olive oil

1 teaspoon sea salt

1. Preheat the oven to 275°F.

2. In a large bowl, use your hands to mix together the kale and olive oil until the kale is evenly coated with the oil.

3. Transfer the kale to a baking sheet, spreading it into a single layer. Sprinkle with the sea salt.

4. Place the sheet in the preheated oven and bake for about 20 minutes, or until the kale is crisp. Turn the chips over halfway through the baking time so both sides crisp.

5. Cool the chips slightly before serving.

• VEGAN
• PALEO
• MEDITERRANEAN

STORAGE TIP: Store the cooled chips in an airtight container at room temperature.

PER SERVING

Calories: 93; Total Fat: 7g; Total Carbohydrates: 7g; Sugar: 0g; Fiber: 1g; Protein: 2g; Sodium: 497mg

Smoked Turkey–Wrapped Zucchini Sticks

SERVES 4 / PREP TIME: 10 MINUTES

· ·

- PALEO
- MEDITERRANEAN
- TIME-SAVING

COOKING TIP: For an added pop of flavor, drizzle with a little olive oil and lemon juice.

PER SERVING
Calories: 137; Total Fat: 3g;
Total Carbohydrates: 6g;
Sugar: 2g; Fiber: 1g;
Protein: 21g; Sodium: 1450mg

The light smokiness of the turkey paired with peppery arugula and the satisfying crunch of a zucchini stick make this a great late-afternoon—or anytime—snack. These travel well, so pack a lunch for work or a picnic. The hit of protein will sustain you longer than anything you get from a vending machine.

8 thin slices smoked turkey
2 zucchini, quartered lengthwise

1 cup packed arugula, divided
Pinch salt

1. Place 1 slice of smoked turkey on a work surface. Top with 1 zucchini stick, ¼ cup of arugula, and a sprinkle of salt.

2. Wrap the turkey around the vegetables and place on a platter seam-side down. Repeat with the remaining ingredients.

3. Cover and chill until ready to serve.

Crunchy-Spicy Chickpeas

MAKES 1 CUP / PREP TIME: 10 MINUTES / COOK TIME: 30 TO 40 MINUTES

A satisfying snack that's easy to store and keep handy for a quick pick-me-up. It's best to eat these within five days since they start to lose their crunch if you keep them longer. Making them yourself is less expensive than buying them, and you also will know exactly what's in them.

1 (15-ounce) can chickpeas, drained

1 teaspoon salt

½ teaspoon ground cumin

½ teaspoon onion powder

½ teaspoon ground turmeric

½ teaspoon chipotle powder

¼ teaspoon garlic powder

2 tablespoons extra-virgin olive oil

1. Preheat the oven to 375°F.
2. Pat the drained chickpeas dry with a paper towel.
3. In a small bowl, stir together the salt, cumin, onion powder, turmeric, chipotle powder, and garlic powder.
4. In a medium bowl, combine the dry chickpeas and olive oil. Gently stir the chickpeas to coat with the oil.
5. Sprinkle the salt mixture over the chickpeas. Stir until coated evenly.
6. On a large baking sheet with raised sides (to keep the chickpeas from rolling off the sheet), spread the chickpeas in a single layer. Place the sheet in the preheated oven and bake for 30 to 40 minutes, stirring occasionally, or until the chickpeas are dry and crunchy.
7. Cool completely before eating.

• VEGAN

• MEDITERRANEAN

STORAGE TIP: If you're not planning on eating these immediately, store in an airtight container at room temperature.

TIME-SAVING TIP: Line the baking sheet with parchment paper before baking the chickpeas. Cleanup will be a snap.

ACTION PLAN TIP: If you're using this recipe as part of the Vegan or Mediterranean Action Plan, double the quantities so you have enough leftovers for later in the week.

PER SERVING (¼ cup) Calories: 192; Total Fat: 10g; Total Carbohydrates: 18g; Sugar: 1g; Fiber: 5g; Protein: 8g; Sodium: 593mg

Sweet Potato Chips

SERVES 4 TO 6 / PREP TIME: 20 MINUTES / COOK TIME: 2 HOURS

• VEGAN

• PALEO

• MEDITERRANEAN

PER SERVING

Calories: 267; Total Fat: 11g;
Total Carbohydrates: 42g;
Sugar: 1g; Fiber: 6g;
Protein: 2g; Sodium: 482mg

Sweet potato chips are absolutely delicious, either alone or with Creamy Broccoli Dip (see page 118). To get a crispy chip, slice the sweet potatoes as thin as possible. Use a mandoline or the thin-slicing disk on a food processor. If all you have is a sharp knife and patience, you're still in luck. Thicker chips are more chewy than crispy, but are every bit as delicious.

2 large sweet potatoes,
  sliced as thin as possible

3 tablespoons extra-virgin
  olive oil

1 teaspoon sea salt

1. Preheat the oven to 250°F.

2. Position the rack in the center of the oven.

3. In a large bowl, toss the sweet potatoes slices with the olive oil. Arrange the slices in a single layer on two baking sheets. Sprinkle with the sea salt.

4. Place the sheets in the preheated oven and bake for about 2 hours, rotating the pans and flipping the chips after 1 hour.

5. Once the chips are lightly brown and crisp, remove them from the oven. Some may be a bit soft, but they will crisp as they cool. Cool the chips for 10 minutes before serving.

6. Serve immediately. The chips lose their crunch within several hours.

Mini Snack Muffins

MAKES 24 / PREP TIME: 20 MINUTES / COOK TIME: 15 TO 20 MINUTES

• MEDITERRANEAN

VEGAN TIP: If
you're following the
Vegan Action Plan,
replace the eggs with
4 teaspoons of ground
flaxseed combined
with 8 ounces of
water.

PALEO TIP: If you're
following the Paleo
Action Plan, replace
the brown rice flour
with coconut flour.

PER SERVING (1 muffin)
Calories: 65; Total Fat: 4g;
Total Carbohydrates: 7g;
Sugar: 1g; Fiber: 1g;
Protein: 2g; Sodium: 66mg

Defend yourself from that snack attack—these muffins have no added sweetener, which makes them a perfect anytime snack. Make ahead to have on hand, or double the batch and store them in the freezer. They are great served warm with a drizzle of raw honey.

¼ cup extra-virgin olive oil,
  plus extra for greasing
1 cup almond flour
1 cup brown rice flour
1 tablespoon baking powder

½ teaspoon salt
1 teaspoon ground cinnamon
4 eggs
1 cup shredded carrot
1 cup canned pumpkin

1. Preheat the oven to 375°F.

2. Line a mini-muffin tin with cupcake liners, or brush the tin with a little olive oil.

3. In a medium bowl, mix together the almond flour, brown rice flour, baking powder, salt, and cinnamon.

4. Add the eggs, carrot, pumpkin, and olive oil. Stir until well combined.

5. Scoop the batter into each muffin cup, filling each three-quarters full.

6. Place the tin in the preheated oven and bake for 15 minutes, or until the muffins are lightly browned. Remove from the oven and cool for 10 minutes before removing the muffins from the tin.

Strawberry-Chia Ice Pops

MAKES 6 ICE POPS / PREP TIME: 20 MINUTES / FREEZE TIME: 5 HOURS

Fresh and refreshing, you can make these ice pops with any frozen or fresh fruit you like. When using fresh fruit, it's best to mash the fruit before combining it with the remaining ingredients. This way you avoid biting into overly large frozen chunks of fruit.

2 cup frozen unsweetened strawberries, thawed

1 tablespoon freshly squeezed lemon juice

1 (15-ounce) can coconut milk

1 tablespoon chia seeds

1 teaspoon vanilla extract

1. Prepare six ice pop molds per the manufacturer's instructions.

2. In a medium bowl, stir together the strawberries, lemon juice, coconut milk, chia seeds, and vanilla. Let the mixture stand for 5 minutes so the chia seeds thicken slightly. This makes it easier to fill the molds.

3. Evenly divide the mixture among the molds. Place 1 ice pop stick in each mold. Freeze the pops for about 5 hours, or overnight, until solid.

• VEGAN
• PALEO
• MEDITERRANEAN

COOKING TIP: If you don't have ice pop molds, use muffin tins instead. Line the tins with parchment paper before filling. Freeze them for 2 hours before inserting sticks, since it's hard to get them to stay upright in the unfrozen mixture.

PER SERVING (1 ice pop)
Calories: 187; Total Fat: 17g; Total Carbohydrates: 9g; Sugar: 6g; Fiber: 3g; Protein: 2g; Sodium: 11mg

7

Soups & Stews

Roasted Vegetable Soup

SERVES 6 TO 8 / PREP TIME: 30 MINUTES / COOK TIME: 40 MINUTES

· ·

- VEGAN
- PALEO
- MEDITERRANEAN

Sensitivity Alert

COOKING TIP: For
a creamy soup, add
½ cup of coconut
milk when you purée
the soup.

TIME-SAVING TIP:
If you're using this
recipe as part of the
Vegan or Paleo Action
Plan, double the
quantities so you have
enough for leftovers
for later in the week.

PER SERVING

Calories: 197; Total Fat: 17g;
Total Carbohydrates: 13g;
Sugar: 5g; Fiber: 3g;
Protein: 2g; Sodium: 426mg

Versatile, vibrant, and very delicious, this recipe works with any vegetables you have on hand. This is a good way to use leftover roasted vegetables or anything in the refrigerator just starting to pass its prime. The roasting adds sweetness and a depth of flavor. Even picky vegetable eaters like this soup.

4 carrots, halved lengthwise

½ head cauliflower, broken
  into florets

2 cups cubed butternut squash

3 shallots, halved lengthwise

3 Roma tomatoes, quartered

4 garlic cloves

½ cup extra-virgin olive oil

1 teaspoon salt

¼ teaspoon freshly ground
  black pepper

4 to 6 cups water or
  vegetable broth

1. Preheat the oven to 400°F.

2. In a large bowl, combine the carrots, cauliflower, butternut squash, shallots, tomatoes, and garlic. Add the olive oil, salt, and pepper and toss the vegetables to coat.

3. On a rimmed baking sheet, arrange the vegetables in a single layer. Place the sheet in the preheated oven, and roast the vegetables for about 25 minutes, or until they start to brown.

4. Transfer the roasted vegetables to a large Dutch oven over high heat. Add enough water to cover the vegetables and bring to a boil. Reduce the heat to a simmer and cook the soup for 10 minutes.

5. Pour the soup into a blender, working in batches if necessary, and purée until smooth.

Mushrooms in Broth

SERVES 4 / PREP TIME: 15 MINUTES / COOK TIME: 10 MINUTES

A soothing soup for a light lunch or snack. Mushrooms have powerful anti-inflammatory benefits and boost our immune systems. Trim a few minutes off your prep time by buying pre-sliced onions and mushrooms and pre-chopped celery.

1 tablespoon extra-virgin olive oil

1 onion, halved and sliced thin

3 garlic cloves, sliced thin

1 celery stalk, finely chopped

1 pound mushrooms, sliced thin

1 teaspoon salt

½ teaspoon freshly ground black pepper

Pinch nutmeg

4 cups vegetable broth

2 tablespoon chopped fresh tarragon

1. In a large pot over high heat, heat the olive oil.

2. Add the onion, garlic, and celery. Sauté for 3 minutes.

3. Add the mushrooms, salt, pepper, and nutmeg. Sauté for 5 to 10 minutes more.

4. Add the vegetable broth and bring the soup to a boil. Reduce the heat to simmer. Cook for an additional 5 minutes.

5. Stir in the tarragon and serve.

- VEGAN
- PALEO
- MEDITERRANEAN

PALEO & MEDITERRANEAN TIP: If following the Mediterranean or Paleo Action Plan, use chicken stock in place of vegetable broth and add 1 cup cooked chicken or fish for a heartier soup.

PER SERVING
Calories: 111; Total Fat: 5g; Total Carbohydrates: 9g; Sugar: 4g; Fiber: 2g; Protein: 9g; Sodium: 1357mg

Fennel, Leek, *and* Pear Soup

SERVES 4 TO 6 / PREP TIME: 15 MINUTES / COOK TIME: 15 MINUTES

- VEGAN
- PALEO
- MEDITERRANEAN

Sensitivity Alert

ACTION PLAN TIP:
If you're using this recipe as part of the Vegan, Paleo, or Mediterranean Action Plan, double the quantities so you have enough leftovers for later in the week.

PER SERVING
Calories: 267; Total Fat: 15g; Total Carbohydrates: 33g; Sugar: 13g; Fiber: 7g; Protein: 5g; Sodium: 627mg

In addition to being restorative and aiding digestion, the fennel and leeks add a mild bite to this soup while the pears add a gentle sweetness. Serve garnished with sliced raw pears and chopped cashews for a nice texture contrast.

2 tablespoons extra-virgin olive oil
2 leeks, white part only, sliced
1 fennel bulb, cut into ¼-inch-thick slices
2 pears, peeled, cored, and cut into ½-inch cubes

1 teaspoon salt
¼ teaspoon freshly ground black pepper
½ cup cashews
3 cups water, or vegetable broth
2 cups packed spinach or arugula

1. In a large Dutch oven over high heat, heat the olive oil.

2. Add the leeks and fennel. Sauté for 5 minutes.

3. Add the pears, salt, and pepper. Sauté for 3 minutes more.

4. Add the cashews and water and bring the soup to a boil. Reduce the heat to simmer and cook for 5 minutes, partially covered.

5. Stir in the spinach.

6. Pour the soup into a blender, working in batches if necessary, and purée until smooth.

Pumpkin Soup
with Fried Sage

SERVES 4 / PREP TIME: 15 MINUTES / COOK TIME: 10 MINUTES

· ·

- VEGAN
- PALEO
- MEDITERRANEAN

INGREDIENT TIP: You can use extra-virgin olive oil to fry the sage leaves, but since the oil is discarded afterward it's better to use a less-expensive oil for this preparation. Sage leaves only stay crisp for several hours, so do not make them too far ahead of time.

ACTION PLAN TIP: If you're using the recipe as part of the Paleo Action Plan, double the quantities so you have enough leftovers for later in the week.

PER SERVING
Calories: 379; Total Fat: 20g; Total Carbohydrates: 45g; Sugar: 17g; Fiber: 18g; Protein: 10g; Sodium: 1365mg

Pumpkin is not just for Thanksgiving anymore. This fast-and-easy soup is made with canned pumpkin, so you can have it whenever the whim hits. You may be tempted to skip the fried sage, but sage has great anti-inflammatory and antioxidant properties; it's also the perfect complement to the pumpkin's earthy flavor.

4 tablespoons extra-virgin olive oil	2 teaspoons chipotle powder
1 onion, chopped	1 teaspoon salt
2 garlic cloves, cut into ⅛-inch-thick slices	½ teaspoon freshly ground black pepper
1 (15-ounce) can pumpkin purée	½ cup vegetable oil
4 cups vegetable broth	12 sage leaves, stemmed

1. In a large, heavy Dutch over high heat, add the olive oil, onion, and garlic. Sauté for about 5 minutes, or until the vegetables begin to brown.

2. Add the pumpkin, vegetable broth, chipotle powder, salt, and pepper. Bring to a boil. Reduce the heat to simmer and cook for 5 minutes.

3. While the soup is simmering, place a medium sauté pan over high heat. Add the vegetable oil and heat until hot.

4. Gently slide each sage leaf into the oil and cook for about 1 minute, or until it crisps. Use a slotted spoon to transfer the sage to paper towels to drain. Once cool, discard the vegetable oil.

5. Ladle the soup into bowls (if desired, first purée the soup in a blender), and garnish each serving with 3 fried sage leaves.

Lentil and Carrot Soup *with* Ginger

SERVES 4 TO 6 / PREP TIME: 15 MINUTES / COOK TIME: 10 MINUTES

Lentils are loaded with protein, iron, and fiber. They pair nicely with ginger, which reduces inflammation and aids digestion. If you're following the Mediterranean Action Plan, garnish the soup with crumbled goat cheese before serving.

1 tablespoon coconut oil

2 carrots, sliced thin

1 small white onion, peeled and sliced thin

2 garlic cloves, peeled and sliced thin

1 tablespoon chopped fresh ginger

3 cups water, or vegetable broth

1 (15-ounce) can lentils, drained and rinsed

2 tablespoons chopped fresh cilantro, or parsley

1 teaspoon salt

¼ teaspoon freshly ground black pepper

- VEGAN
- MEDITERRANEAN

ACTION PLAN TIP:
If you're using this recipe as part of the Vegan or Mediterranean Action Plan, double the quantities so you have enough leftovers for later in the week.

PER SERVING

Calories: 207; Total Fat: 5g;
Total Carbohydrates: 28g;
Sugar: 5g; Fiber: 10g;
Protein: 14g; Sodium: 1430mg

1. In a large pot over medium-high heat, melt the coconut oil. Add the carrots, onion, garlic, and ginger. Sauté for 5 minutes.

2. Add the water to the pot and bring to a boil. Reduce the heat to simmer and cook for about 5 minutes, or until the carrots are tender.

3. Add the lentils, cilantro, salt, and pepper. Stir well, and serve.

Coconut Curry–Butternut Squash Soup

SERVES 4 TO 6 / PREP TIME: 15 MINUTES / COOK TIME: 4 HOURS

- VEGAN
- PALEO
- MEDITERRANEAN
- TIME-SAVING

ACTION PLAN TIP:
If you're using this recipe as part of the Vegan, Paleo, or Time-Saving Action Plan, double the quantities so you have enough leftovers for later in the week.

PER SERVING
Calories: 416; Total Fat: 31g; Total Carbohydrates: 30g; Sugar: 13g; Fiber: 7g; Protein: 10g; Sodium: 1387mg

This soup is made in the slow cooker: Load the ingredients in the morning and come home to a fragrant house and a ready-to-eat meal. Dress up the soup with garnishes like shredded coconut, chopped cashews, and diced green apple.

2 tablespoons coconut oil

1 pound butternut squash, peeled and cut into 1-inch cubes

1 small head cauliflower, cut into 1-inch pieces

1 onion, sliced

1 tablespoon curry powder

½ cup no-added-sugar apple juice

4 cups vegetable broth

1 (13.5-ounce) can coconut milk

1 teaspoon salt

¼ teaspoon freshly ground white pepper

¼ cup chopped fresh cilantro, divided

1. In the slower cooker, combine the coconut oil, butternut squash, cauliflower, onion, curry powder, apple juice, vegetable broth, coconut milk, salt, and white pepper. Set on high for 4 hours.

2. Serve the soup as is or purée it in a blender before serving.

3. Garnish with the cilantro.

Soba Noodle Soup
with Spinach

SERVES 4 / PREP TIME: 15 MINUTES / COOK TIME: 10 MINUTES

Look for 100 percent buckwheat soba noodles as any that contain gluten are not anti-inflammatory. Buckwheat soba noodles cook quickly and are good served hot or cold. If you can't find shiitake mushrooms, or they are too costly, substitute another type of mushroom.

2 tablespoons coconut oil

8 ounces shiitake mushrooms, stemmed and sliced thin

4 scallions, sliced thin

1 garlic clove, minced

1 tablespoon minced fresh ginger

1 teaspoon salt

4 cups vegetable broth

3 cups water

4 ounces buckwheat soba noodles

1 bunch spinach, washed and cut into strips

1 tablespoon freshly squeezed lemon juice

• VEGAN

• MEDITERRANEAN

ACTION PLAN TIP:
If you're using this recipe as part of the Vegan or Mediterranean Action Plan, double the quantities so you have enough for leftovers for later in the week.

PER SERVING
Calories: 255; Total Fat: 9g;
Total Carbohydrates: 34g;
Sugar: 4g; Fiber: 4g;
Protein: 13g; Sodium: 1774mg

1. In a large pot over medium heat, heat the coconut oil.

2. Add the mushrooms, scallions, garlic, ginger, and salt. Sauté for 5 minutes.

3. Add the vegetable broth and water to the pot and bring to a boil. Add the soba noodles and cook for 5 minutes.

4. Remove the pot from the heat. Stir in the spinach and lemon juice. Serve hot.

Sweet Potato *and* Rice Soup

SERVES 4 TO 6 / PREP TIME: 15 MINUTES / COOK TIME: 15 MINUTES

This simple and soothing soup could be called "leftover soup" because it's great to make with leftover rice and vegetables. The soup is very mild in flavor; spice it up with red pepper flakes or a teaspoon or two of coconut aminos.

4 cups vegetable broth

1 large sweet potato, peeled and cut into 1-inch cubes

2 onions, coarsely chopped

2 garlic cloves, sliced thin

2 teaspoons minced fresh ginger

1 bunch broccolini, cut into 1-inch pieces

1 cup cooked basmati rice

¼ cup fresh cilantro leaves

1. In a large Dutch oven over high heat, add the broth and bring to a boil.

2. Add the sweet potato, onion, garlic, and ginger. Simmer for 5 to 8 minutes, or until the sweet potato is cooked through.

3. Add the broccolini and simmer for an additional 3 minutes.

4. Remove the pan from the heat. Stir in the rice and cilantro.

• VEGAN

MEDITERRANEAN & PALEO TIP: If following the Mediterranean or Paleo Action Plans, use chicken broth instead of vegetable. If following the Paleo Action Plan, omit the rice, too.

PER SERVING

Calories: 167; Total Fat: 2g; Total Carbohydrates: 29g; Sugar: 7g; Fiber: 3g; Protein: 8g; Sodium: 789mg

Broccoli *and* Lentil Stew

SERVES 4 / PREP TIME: 15 MINUTES / COOK TIME: 30 MINUTES

• VEGAN

• MEDITERRANEAN

PER SERVING
Calories: 182; Total Fat: 6g;
Total Carbohydrates: 24g;
Sugar: 5g; Fiber: 9g;
Protein: 11g; Sodium: 1233mg

Green olives and Italian parsley give this stew its Mediterranean flavors. The broccoli and lentils are loaded with fiber and make this stew hearty. This is a good meal to warm you on a cold day.

1 tablespoon extra-virgin olive oil, plus additional for drizzling

1 small onion, finely chopped

1 small carrot, chopped

2 cloves garlic, minced

2 cups vegetable broth

1 cup dried green or brown lentils

1 teaspoon dried oregano

6 cups broccoli florets

1 teaspoon salt

¼ teaspoon freshly ground black pepper

½ cup sliced pitted green olives

¼ cup chopped fresh Italian parsley

1. In a large pot over high heat, heat the olive oil.

2. Add the onion, carrot, and garlic. Sauté for 5 minutes.

3. Add the vegetable broth, lentils, and oregano and bring to a boil. Reduce the heat to simmer. Cook the soup for 15 to 20 minutes, or until the lentils are tender.

4. Add the broccoli, cover the pot, and simmer for 5 minutes more.

5. Remove the pot from the heat and stir in the olives and parsley. If the soup is too thick, stir in some water.

6. Ladle the soup into bowls, drizzle with a little olive oil, and serve.

Winter Squash *and* Kasha Stew

SERVES 4 / PREP TIME: 15 MINUTES / COOK TIME: 4 HOURS

Kasha is toasted buckwheat. It is not a grain; it is actually a grass. It's thick and hearty and is good combined with winter squash. The kale is added at the end of the cooking time to preserve its texture and nutrition. As with most greens, it loses more of its nutrients the longer it cooks. This soup will both comfort and nourish you.

- 1 tablespoon extra-virgin olive oil
- 2 pounds winter squash, peeled and cubed
- 1 fennel bulb, sliced thin
- 2 leeks, white part only, sliced thin
- 2 garlic cloves, chopped
- 1 cup kasha, rinsed
- 1 teaspoon salt
- ½ teaspoon freshly ground black pepper
- 3 cups water, or vegetable broth
- 4 cups chopped kale, thoroughly washed and stemmed

1. In the slow cooker, combine the olive oil, squash, fennel, leeks, garlic, kasha, salt, pepper, and water. Set the cooker on high for 4 hours.

2. Just before serving, stir in the kale. The heat from the stew will wilt it, making it easy to chew and digest.

- VEGAN
- MEDITERRANEAN
- TIME-SAVING

PALEO TIP: Omit the kasha and replace the water or vegetable broth with chicken broth. Add 1 pound mild Italian turkey sausage cut into 1-inch slices to the slow cooker with the rest of the ingredients.

ACTION PLAN TIP: If you're using this recipe as part of the Vegan, Mediterranean, or Time-Saving Action Plan, double the quantities so you have enough for leftovers for later in the week.

PER SERVING

Calories: 325; Total Fat: 6g; Total Carbohydrates: 60g; Sugar: 2g; Fiber: 8g; Protein: 12g; Sodium: 1231mg

Chicken Chili *with* Beans

SERVES 6 / PREP TIME: 15 MINUTES / COOK TIME: 4 HOURS

- MEDITERRANEAN
- TIME-SAVING

Sensitivity Alert

VEGAN TIP: If you're following the Vegan Action Plan, omit the chicken and use vegetable broth instead of chicken broth.

PER SERVING

Calories: 423; Total Fat: 13g; Total Carbohydrates: 41g; Sugar: 6g; Fiber: 10g; Protein: 42g; Sodium: 857mg

Chicken chili is a family favorite, and it can be especially filling when served over brown rice or cooked quinoa. The small amount of chipotle powder provides an ever-so-small kick of heat but not too much for those who don't like their food too spicy. This recipe doubles (or triples!) easily. Freeze extra portions in single-serving containers for a quick meal or to take to work for lunches.

2 tablespoons extra-virgin olive oil

2 onions, chopped

4 garlic cloves, minced

2 celery stalks, chopped

2 teaspoons ground cumin

1 teaspoon salt

1 teaspoon chipotle powder

½ teaspoon freshly ground black pepper

4 boneless skinless chicken breasts, cut into 1-inch pieces

1 teaspoon dried oregano

1 bay leaf

1 (28-ounce) can chopped tomatoes

2½ cups chicken broth, plus additional as needed

2 (15-ounce) cans white beans, drained and rinsed

¼ cup chopped fresh parsley, divided

1. In the slow cooker, combine the olive oil, onions, garlic, celery, cumin, salt, chipotle powder, pepper, chicken, oregano, bay leaf, tomatoes, chicken broth, and white beans. Set to high and cook for 4 hours.

2. If the mixture gets too thick, add a little more chicken broth or some water.

3. Garnish each serving with parsley. Serve alone or over cooked brown rice or quinoa.

Mango *and* Black Bean Stew

SERVES 4 / PREP TIME: 10 MINUTES / COOK TIME: 10 MINUTES

· VEGAN

· MEDITERRANEAN

ACTION PLAN TIP:
If you're using this recipe as part of the Vegan Action Plan, double the quantities so you have enough leftovers for later in the week.

PER SERVING
Calories: 431; Total Fat: 9g;
Total Carbohydrates: 72g;
Sugar: 17g; Fiber: 22g;
Protein: 20g; Sodium: 609mg

Mangos alkalize in your body and have enzymes that aid digestion. This stew is super-simple and super-fast—and really delicious. Leftovers can be used as a condiment on grilled poultry or seafood—and, of course, on their own.

2 tablespoons coconut oil

1 onion, chopped

2 (15-ounce) cans black beans, drained and rinsed

1 tablespoon chili powder

1 teaspoon salt

¼ teaspoon freshly ground black pepper

1 cup water

2 ripe mangos, sliced thin

¼ cup chopped fresh cilantro, divided

¼ cup sliced scallions, divided

1. In a large pot over high heat, melt the coconut oil.

2. Add the onion and sauté for 5 minutes.

3. Add the black beans, chili powder, salt, pepper, and water. Bring to a boil. Reduce the heat to simmer and cook for 5 minutes.

4. Remove the pot from the heat; stir in the mangos just before serving. Garnish each serving with the cilantro and scallions.

Coconut Fish Stew

SERVES 4 / PREP TIME: 15 MINUTES / COOK TIME: 10 MINUTES

This dish adds an exotic touch to your Action Plan. Lemongrass is used in many Pacific Rim recipes. It aids digestion and is reported to lower blood pressure. It has a light lemony flavor that brightens the flavor of other ingredients. Here it is bruised to release its essential oils while simmering in the broth. Don't forget to remove the stalk before serving.

2 tablespoons coconut oil

1 white onion, sliced thin

2 garlic cloves, sliced thin

2 zucchini, sliced thin

1½ pounds firm white fish fillet, cut into 1-inch cubes

1 (4-inch) piece lemongrass (white part only), bruised with the back of a knife

1 (13.5-ounce) can coconut milk

1 teaspoon salt

¼ teaspoon freshly ground white pepper

½ cup slivered scallions

¼ cup chopped cilantro

3 tablespoons freshly squeezed lemon juice

1. In a large pot over medium heat, melt the coconut oil.

2. Add the onion, garlic, and zucchini. Sauté for 5 minutes.

3. Add the fish, lemongrass, coconut milk, salt, and white pepper to the pot. If the liquid doesn't cover the fish, add enough water to do so. Bring to a boil, then reduce the heat to simmer, and cook for 5 minutes.

4. Garnish the soup with the scallions, cilantro, and lemon juice.

• PALEO

• MEDITERRANEAN

COOKING TIP: If you like it spicy, add 1 teaspoon of red pepper flakes.

PALEO TIP: If you're following the Paleo Action Plan, replace the beans with 2 cups each cubed zucchini and cauliflower.

ACTION PLAN TIP: If you're using this recipe as part of the Mediterranean or Time-Saving Action Plan, double the quantities so you have enough leftovers for later in the week.

PER SERVING

Calories: 608; Total Fat: 43g; Total Carbohydrates: 13g; Sugar: 7g; Fiber: 4g; Protein: 46g; Sodium: 725mg

8

Salads & Sides

Sliced Apple, Beet, and Celery Salad

SERVES 4 / PREP TIME: 15 MINUTES

- VEGAN
- PALEO
- MEDITERRANEAN
- TIME-SAVING

VEGAN TIP: If you're following the Vegan Action Plan, use the maple syrup in place of the honey.

ACTION PLAN TIP: If you're using this recipe as part of the Vegan, Paleo, or Time-Saving Action Plan, double the quantities so you have enough for leftovers for later in the week.

PER SERVING
Calories: 239; Total Fat: 15g; Total Carbohydrates: 27g; Sugar: 18g; Fiber: 5g; Protein: 4g; Sodium: 121mg

If you think you don't like beets, you haven't tried this salad. If there are any leftovers, the other ingredients will likely turn the same color as the beets. No need to worry, it's still perfectly fine to eat. The best way to slice the vegetables is with a mandoline, but the slicing disk of a food processor works well, too.

2 green apples, cored and quartered

2 small beets, peeled and quartered

4 cups spinach

2 celery stalks, sliced thin

½ red onion, sliced thin

½ cup shredded carrots

1 tablespoon apple cider vinegar

1 tablespoon raw honey or maple syrup

3 tablespoons extra-virgin olive oil

Salt

Freshly ground black pepper

¼ cup pumpkin seeds

1. Using a mandoline or the slicing disk of a food processor, slice the apples and the beets.

2. Place the spinach on a large platter. Arrange the apples and beets over the spinach. Top with the celery, red onion, and carrots.

3. In a small bowl, whisk together the cider vinegar, honey, and olive oil. Season with salt and pepper.

4. Drizzle the dressing over the salad and garnish with the pumpkin seeds.

Avocado *and* Mango Salad

SERVES 4 / PREP TIME: 15 MINUTES

This is a light, refreshing salad loaded with healthy fats and fiber. For crunch, garnish it with toasted slivered almonds and shredded coconut. If you want to experiment with different foods in the morning, this makes an excellent breakfast salad.

2 romaine lettuce hearts, chopped

1 cucumber, peeled and cut into ¼-inch cubes

2 ripe mangos, cut into ½-inch cubes

2 scallions, sliced thin

1 large ripe avocado

1 cup Creamy Coconut-Herb Dressing (page 252)

1. In a large serving bowl, combine the romaine lettuce, cucumber, mangos, scallions, and avocado.

2. Pour the Creamy Coconut-Herb Dressing over the fruit and vegetables. Toss to combine.

• VEGAN
• PALEO
• MEDITERRANEAN
• TIME-SAVING

PALEO & MEDITERRANEAN TIP:
For those following the Mediterranean and Paleo Action Plans, add grilled chicken or fish to make this an entrée salad.

PER SERVING

Calories: 253; Total Fat: 13g; Total Carbohydrates: 37g; Sugar: 21g; Fiber: 10g; Protein: 4g; Sodium: 363mg

Almost Caesar Salad

SERVES 4 / PREP TIME: 15 MINUTES

• PALEO

• MEDITERRANEAN

• TIME-SAVING

VEGAN TIP: If you're following the Vegan Action Plan, substitute olives for the anchovies when making the Almost Caesar Dressing (page 256).

PALEO & MEDITERRANEAN TIP: For those following the Mediterranean and Paleo Action Plans, add grilled chicken to make this an entrée salad.

PER SERVING
Calories: 431; Total Fat: 42g; Total Carbohydrates: 14g; Sugar: 3g; Fiber: 5g; Protein: 6g; Sodium: 803mg

Caesar salad served in a restaurant is undoubtedly loaded with croutons, eggs, and shaved Parmesan cheese. This version keeps the authentic flavors of a Caesar but without all the inflammation-causing foods. Hearts of palm add a nice tang, and the crunch of the sunflower seeds replaces the croutons.

2 romaine lettuce hearts, chopped

1 (14-ounce) can hearts of palm, drained and sliced

½ cup sunflower seeds

1 recipe Almost Caesar Dressing (page 256)

Salt

Freshly ground black pepper

1. In a large bowl, combine the romaine lettuce, hearts of palm, and sunflower seeds.

2. Add enough dressing to lightly coat the lettuce leaves. Reserve any remaining dressing for another use.

3. Season the salad with salt and pepper, and serve.

Brussels Sprout Slaw

SERVES 4 / PREP TIME: 15 MINUTES

Many people grew up hating those oft-overcooked Brussels sprouts that were supposedly "good for you." If you're one of those people, this is the way to eat them. This crunchy slaw makes a wonderful side dish to roasted chicken or turkey. If pomegranate seeds aren't available, substitute dried cherries.

1 pound Brussels sprouts, stem ends removed and sliced thin

½ red onion, sliced thin

1 apple, cored and sliced thin

1 teaspoon Dijon mustard

1 teaspoon salt

1 tablespoon raw honey or maple syrup

2 teaspoons apple cider vinegar

1 cup plain coconut milk yogurt

½ cup chopped toasted hazelnuts

½ cup pomegranate seeds

1. In a medium bowl, combine the Brussels sprouts, onion, and apple.

2. In a small bowl, whisk together the Dijon mustard, salt, honey, cider vinegar, and yogurt.

3. Add the dressing to the Brussels sprouts and toss until evenly coated.

4. Garnish the salad with the hazelnuts and pomegranate seeds.

- VEGAN
- PALEO
- MEDITERRANEAN
- TIME-SAVING

Sensitivity Alert

COOKING TIP: The flavor of this slaw improves if it sits for 30 minutes before serving.

VEGAN TIP: If you're following the Vegan Action Plan, use the maple syrup instead of the honey.

PER SERVING

Calories: 189; Total Fat: 8g; Total Carbohydrates: 29g; Sugar: 13g; Fiber: 9g; Protein: 6g; Sodium: 678mg

Vegetable Slaw
with Feta Cheese

SERVES 4 TO 6 / PREP TIME: 20 MINUTES

• VEGAN

• MEDITERRANEAN

VEGAN &
PALEO TIP: Omit the feta cheese; if you choose, use cashew cheese instead.

VEGAN TIP: If you're following the Vegan Action Plan, use the maple syrup instead of the honey.

PER SERVING

Calories: 388; Total Fat: 30g; Total Carbohydrates: 26g; Sugar: 12g; Fiber: 6g; Protein: 8g; Sodium: 981mg

This slaw is a great way to get your vegetables. Shredded broccoli, carrots, celery root, beets, zucchini, and red onions make this a colorful and antioxidant-rich slaw. A food processor shredding disk makes short work of the prep. Make this slaw with any vegetables you like.

½ cup extra-virgin olive oil

½ cup apple cider vinegar

1 tablespoon raw honey or maple syrup

1 teaspoon Dijon mustard

1 teaspoon salt

¼ teaspoon freshly ground black pepper

2 large broccoli stems, peeled and shredded

2 carrots, peeled and shredded

½ celery root bulb, peeled and shredded

1 large beet, peeled and shredded

2 zucchini, shredded

1 small red onion, sliced thin

¼ cup chopped fresh Italian parsley

3 ounces feta cheese, crumbled

1. In a large bowl, whisk together the olive oil, cider vinegar, honey, Dijon mustard, salt, and pepper.

2. Add the broccoli, carrots, celery root, beets, zucchini, onion, and Italian parsley. Toss to coat the vegetables with the dressing.

3. Transfer the slaw to a serving bowl and garnish with the feta cheese.

Mediterranean Chopped Salad

SERVES 4 / PREP TIME: 15 MINUTES

• VEGAN
• PALEO
• MEDITERRANEAN
• TIME-SAVING

PALEO & MEDITERRANEAN TIP: To make this an entrée salad on the Mediterranean or Paleo Action Plans, add cooked chicken or fish.

MEDITERRANEAN TIP: If following the Mediterranean Action Plan, crumble 3 ounces of goat cheese on top.

ACTION PLAN TIP: If you're using this recipe as part of the Vegan, Paleo, Mediterranean, or Time-Saving Action Plan, double the quantities so you have enough leftovers for later in the week.

PER SERVING
Calories: 194; Total Fat: 14g; Total Carbohydrates: 15g; Sugar: 7g; Fiber: 5g; Protein: 4g; Sodium: 661mg

Inspired by fattoush, a salad of flatbread and vegetables, this version has everything but the flatbread. Sumac, a Middle Eastern spice, is a traditional ingredient in this salad. It has a slight lemony flavor. The salad is very refreshing and pairs nicely with lamb. For added protein, you can add drained garbanzo beans or white beans.

2 cups packed spinach
3 large tomatoes, diced
1 bunch radishes, sliced thin
1 English cucumber, peeled and diced
2 scallions, sliced
2 garlic cloves, minced
1 tablespoon chopped fresh mint
1 tablespoon chopped fresh parsley

1 cup unsweetened plain almond yogurt
¼ cup extra-virgin olive oil
3 tablespoons freshly squeezed lemon juice
1 tablespoon apple cider vinegar
1 teaspoon salt
¼ teaspoon freshly ground black pepper
1 tablespoon sumac

In a large bowl, combine the spinach, tomatoes, radishes, cucumber, scallions, garlic, mint, parsley, yogurt, olive oil, lemon juice, cider vinegar, salt, pepper, and sumac. Toss to combine.

Quinoa *and* Roasted Asparagus Salad

SERVES 4 / PREP TIME: 10 MINUTES / COOK TIME: 15 MINUTES

This dish is guaranteed to become a favorite. Make it even easier using precooked quinoa, available in the frozen-food section of many grocery stores. Roasting the asparagus intensifies its flavor; the flaxseed adds crunch and nuttiness to the salad.

• VEGAN
• MEDITERRANEAN

PER SERVING
Calories: 228; Total Fat: 13g;
Total Carbohydrates: 24g;
Sugar: 2g; Fiber: 5g;
Protein: 6g; Sodium: 592mg

1 bunch asparagus, trimmed

3 tablespoons extra-virgin
 olive oil, divided

1 teaspoon salt, plus additional
 for seasoning

2 cups cooked quinoa,
 cold or at room temperature

¼ red onion, finely chopped

1 tablespoon apple cider vinegar

¼ cup chopped fresh mint

1 tablespoon flaxseed

Freshly ground black pepper

1. Preheat the oven to 400°F.

2. In a large bowl, toss the asparagus with 1 tablespoon
   of olive oil and 1 teaspoon of salt.

3. Wrap the asparagus in aluminum foil in a single layer
   and place the pouch on a baking sheet. Place the sheet
   in the preheated oven and roast the asparagus for 10 to
   15 minutes.

4. While the asparagus is roasting, mix together the quinoa,
   onion, vinegar, mint, flaxseed, and the remaining 2 tablespoons of olive oil in a large bowl.

5. Once the asparagus is cool enough to handle, slice it into
   ½-inch pieces. Add them to the quinoa and season with
   salt and pepper.

White Bean *and* Tuna Salad

SERVES 4 / PREP TIME: 15 MINUTES

• MEDITERRANEAN

• TIME-SAVING

PALEO TIP: Omit the white beans and feta cheese.

ACTION PLAN TIP: If you're using this recipe as part of the Time-Saving Action Plan, double the quantities so you have enough for leftovers for later in the week.

PER SERVING

Calories: 373; Total Fat: 19g; Total Carbohydrates: 28g; Sugar: 3g; Fiber: 7g; Protein: 29g; Sodium: 388mg

This is a "pantry salad," since it's likely all the ingredients are part of your well-stocked pantry. The flavors in this salad improve even more if you make it ahead of time. If making it ahead, don't add the tomatoes and arugula until just before serving.

4 cups arugula

2 (5-ounce) cans flaked white tuna, drained

1 (15-ounce) can white beans, drained and rinsed

½ pint cherry tomatoes, halved lengthwise

½ red onion, finely chopped

½ cup pitted Kalamata olives

¼ cup extra-virgin olive oil

2 tablespoons freshly squeezed lemon juice

Salt

Freshly ground black pepper

2 ounces crumbled sheep's milk or goat's milk feta cheese

1. In a large bowl, mix together the arugula, tuna, white beans, tomatoes, onion, olives, olive oil, and lemon juice. Season with salt and pepper.

2. Just before serving, top the salad with the feta cheese.

Mango Salsa

MAKES ABOUT 2 CUPS / PREP TIME: 15 MINUTES

This salsa will enliven almost any dish—or party. It's good on fish, chicken, tacos, and salads. The mangos have vitamins A and C and probiotic fiber. Substitute papaya for the mangos, or make this with a combination of the two.

- VEGAN
- PALEO
- MEDITERRANEAN
- TIME-SAVING

2 cups chopped mango
½ cup minced red onion
¼ cup chopped fresh cilantro
1 garlic clove, minced

1 tablespoon freshly squeezed
  lemon juice
Pinch salt

PER SERVING (¼ cup)
Calories: 40; Total Fat: 0g;
Total Carbohydrates: 10g;
Sugar: 8g; Fiber: 1g;
Protein: 0g; Sodium: 98mg

1. In a medium bowl, stir together the mango, onion, cilantro, garlic, lemon juice, and salt.

2. Refrigerate in an airtight container for up to one week.

Roasted Root Vegetables

SERVES 4 TO 6 / PREP TIME: 15 MINUTES / COOK TIME: 25 TO 35 MINUTES

Roasting root vegetables is an easy way to get even the pickiest eaters to eat them. The vegetables become sweeter and more intensely flavored, and the outsides are slightly crispy, brown, and delicious. Any leftovers can be turned into Roasted Vegetable Soup (page 130).

2 small sweet potatoes, peeled and cut into 1-inch cubes

1 bunch beets, peeled and cut into 1-inch cubes

4 carrots, peeled and cut into 1-inch rounds

3 parsnips, peeled and cut into 1-inch rounds

¼ cup coconut oil, melted

1 tablespoon extra-virgin olive oil

1 tablespoon raw honey, or maple syrup

1 teaspoon salt

½ teaspoon freshly ground black pepper

1. Preheat the oven to 400°F.

2. Line two rimmed baking sheets with parchment paper.

3. In a large bowl, combine the sweet potatoes, beets, carrots, and parsnips. Add the coconut oil, olive oil, honey, salt, and pepper. Toss to coat the vegetables.

4. Divide the vegetables between the two baking sheets, spreading them into a single layer.

5. Place the sheets in the preheated oven and bake the vegetables for 10 to 15 minutes. Turn them so they brown on the other side. Continue to bake the vegetables for 10 to 15 minutes more, or until brown and tender. Serve warm or at room temperature.

- VEGAN
- PALEO
- MEDITERRANEAN

COOKING TIP: If the vegetables are brown but not quite cooked through, remove them from the oven. Cover the pans with aluminum foil and let the vegetables steam for about 10 minutes. Also, the fresher the vegetables, the less time needed to roast them.

VEGAN TIP: If you're following the Vegan Action Plan, use the maple syrup instead of the honey.

PER SERVING

Calories: 460; Total Fat: 18g; Total Carbohydrates: 74g; Sugar: 23g; Fiber: 14g; Protein: 6g; Sodium: 760mg

Turmeric Chicken Salad

SERVES 4 / PREP TIME: 15 MINUTES / COOK TIME: 20 MINUTES

• PALEO

• MEDITERRANEAN

• TIME-SAVING

Sensitivity Alert

TIME-SAVER TIP: The chicken can be cooked a day ahead and served cold over the salad.

VEGAN TIP: Instead of chicken, mix the olive oil, cilantro, garlic, salt, turmeric, and pepper with a can of drained garbanzo or white beans and serve over the yogurt-dressed greens.

PER SERVING

Calories: 418; Total Fat: 21g;
Total Carbohydrates: 10g;
Sugar: 3g; Fiber: 4g;
Protein: 46g; Sodium: 759mg

Turmeric, used here in the spice rub for the chicken, is a powerful anti-inflammatory. This rub is also delicious on salmon, which you could use in place of the chicken. Marinate it for at least 30 minutes, or overnight, for the best flavor.

4 boneless skinless
  chicken breasts

1 tablespoon extra-virgin
  olive oil

1 tablespoon chopped
  fresh cilantro

1 garlic clove, minced

1 teaspoon salt

¼ teaspoon ground turmeric

¼ teaspoon freshly ground
  black pepper

½ cup plain unsweetened
  almond yogurt

1 tablespoon freshly squeezed
  lemon juice

1 teaspoon lemon zest

½ cup chopped almonds

6 cups chopped romaine lettuce

1. In a shallow baking dish, place the chicken breast.

2. In a small bowl, whisk together the olive oil, cilantro, garlic, salt, turmeric, and pepper. Rub the mixture all over the chicken. Cover the chicken and marinate, refrigerated, for at least 30 minutes, or overnight.

3. Preheat the oven to 375°F. When the oven is hot, place the baking dish in the preheated oven and bake the chicken for 20 minutes. Remove from the oven and set aside.

4. In a large bowl, whisk together the yogurt, lemon juice, and lemon zest. Add the almonds and romaine lettuce and toss to coat the lettuce with the dressing.

5. Transfer the salad to a serving platter. Slice the chicken breasts into strips and arrange them over lettuce.

Lentil, Vegetable, *and* Fruit Bowl

SERVES 4 TO 6 / PREP TIME: 20 MINUTES

A refreshing twist on the typical brown rice and lentil combination. Fresh-tasting and crunchy red lentils, soaked overnight, are paired with jicama and pear here. The base for this salad can be made the night before and the fruits and vegetables added the next day.

- VEGAN
- MEDITERRANEAN

PER SERVING
Calories: 989; Total Fat: 31g;
Total Carbohydrates: 151g;
Sugar: 16g; Fiber: 35g;
Protein: 31g; Sodium: 272mg

1 cup red lentils

2 cups water

4 cups cooked brown rice

1 (15-ounce) can lentils, drained and rinsed

Chicken Lettuce Wraps sauce (page 212)

1 head radicchio, cored and torn into pieces, divided

1 small jicama, peeled and cut into thin sticks, divided

2 red Bartlett (or other) ripe pears, cored, quartered, and sliced, divided

2 scallions, sliced, divided

1. In a medium bowl, combine the red lentils and the water. Cover and refrigerate overnight. Drain the lentils when ready to prepare the salad.

2. In a medium bowl, combine the brown rice and canned lentils. Stir in half of the Chicken Lettuce Wraps sauce. Let the mixture stand for at least 30 minutes, or overnight.

3. Divide the lentil-rice mixture among serving bowls. Top each bowl with equal amounts of the soaked and drained red lentils. Garnish each serving with the radicchio, jicama, pears, and scallions.

4. Drizzle each with some of the remaining Chicken Lettuce Wraps sauce.

Roasted Cauliflower *with* Almond Sauce

SERVES 4 / PREP TIME: 15 MINUTES / COOK TIME: 20 MINUTES

• VEGAN

• PALEO

• MEDITERRANEAN

COOKING TIP: If pomegranate seeds are in season, they make a great garnish.

PER SERVING
Calories: 277; Total Fat: 23g; Total Carbohydrates: 15g; Sugar: 6g; Fiber: 4g; Protein: 7g; Sodium: 945mg

Roasting cauliflower makes it tender on the inside with crunchy bits on the outside. Adding almond sauce makes it delectable. This can be served warm or cold and as a side dish or salad.

1 head cauliflower, cut into florets

¼ cup extra-virgin olive oil

½ teaspoon ground turmeric

1½ teaspoons salt, divided

½ teaspoon freshly ground black pepper, divided

1 cup plain unsweetened almond yogurt

¼ cup almond butter

1 scallion, sliced

1 garlic clove, minced

1 tablespoon chopped fresh parsley

1 tablespoon freshly squeezed lemon juice

1 tablespoon maple syrup

1. Preheat the oven to 400°F.

2. In a large bowl, mix together the cauliflower, olive oil, turmeric, 1 teaspoon of salt, and ¼ teaspoon of pepper.

3. Transfer the seasoned cauliflower to a rimmed baking sheet, placing it in a single layer. Place the sheet in the preheated oven and roast for 20 to 30 minutes, or until the cauliflower is lightly browned and tender.

4. In a blender, combine the yogurt, almond butter, scallions, garlic, parsley, lemon juice, maple syrup, the remaining ½ teaspoon of salt, and the remaining ¼ teaspoon of pepper. Purée until smooth.

5. Place the roasted cauliflower in a serving dish and spoon the almond sauce over it.

Cauliflower Purée

SERVES 4 / PREP TIME: 15 MINUTES / COOK TIME: 10 MINUTES

Cauliflower purée is a great substitute for mashed potatoes, and goes nicely with grilled seafood and meat. This makes a great side dish to accompany roasted vegetables and you can use it to make a vegan soup. Make a double batch and freeze the extras for a quick add-on for dinner.

- VEGAN
- PALEO
- MEDITERRANEAN

1 head cauliflower, broken into florets

1 garlic clove

2 teaspoons salt, divided

¼ teaspoon freshly ground black pepper

½ cup coconut milk

1 tablespoon extra-virgin olive oil

1. Bring a large pot of water to a boil over high heat. Add the cauliflower, garlic clove, and 1 teaspoon of salt. Boil for about 5 minutes, or until the cauliflower is tender.

2. Drain the cauliflower with the garlic clove and transfer to a large bowl. Mash with a potato masher.

3. Add the remaining 1 teaspoon of salt, the pepper, and coconut milk to the mash. Stir until well combined.

4. Place the purée in a serving bowl and drizzle with olive oil.

COOKING TIP: For a smooth-textured purée, place the cooked cauliflower, garlic, salt, pepper, and coconut milk in a food processor and process until smooth.

PER SERVING

Calories: 117; Total Fat: 11g; Total Carbohydrates: 6g; Sugar: 3g; Fiber: 2g; Protein: 2g; Sodium: 1187mg

Green Beans
with Crispy Shallots

SERVES 4 / PREP TIME: 10 MINUTES / COOK TIME: 15 MINUTES

• VEGAN

• PALEO

• MEDITERRANEAN

PER SERVING

Calories: 146; Total Fat: 13g;
Total Carbohydrates: 9g;
Sugar: 2g; Fiber: 4g;
Protein: 2g; Sodium: 475mg

As the shallots crisp in the oil they infuse the beans with their delicious, delicate allium flavor. This recipe is a perfect side dish to any entrée and will make your dinner that much more special.

1 teaspoon sea salt, plus additional for seasoning

1 pound green beans, trimmed

¼ cup extra-virgin olive oil

1 large shallot, sliced thin

1 tablespoon chopped fresh tarragon

Freshly ground black pepper

1. Bring a large pot of water to a boil over high heat.

2. Add 1 teaspoon of sea salt to the boiling water and add the beans to the pot. Cook for about 5 minutes, or until they turn bright green.

3. Drain the beans and transfer them to a serving dish.

4. In a small pan over medium heat, heat the olive oil. Once the oil is hot, add the shallots. Cook for 1 to 2 minutes, or until they start to brown.

5. Spoon the shallots over the green beans. Sprinkle with the tarragon and season with sea salt and pepper.

Roasted Sweet Potatoes *and* Pineapple

SERVES 4 / PREP TIME: 15 MINUTES / COOK TIME: 25 MINUTES

This dish is culinary yin and yang. Curry powder seasons the sweet potatoes and roasting them with the pineapple brings out the best flavors in the curry powder. Sweet, juicy pineapple packs plenty of vitamin C and aids digestion. This makes a light meal on its own and is wonderful paired with chicken, salmon, or swordfish.

3 tablespoons coconut oil

2 large sweet potatoes, or yams, peeled and cut into ½-inch pieces

1 cup fresh pineapple, cut into ½-inch pieces

2 teaspoons curry powder

1 teaspoon salt

¼ teaspoon freshly ground black pepper

1. Preheat the oven to 400°F.

2. In a microwave-safe bowl, melt the coconut oil in the microwave on high for about 1 minute.

3. In a large bowl, combine the sweet potatoes and pineapple. Add the melted coconut oil, curry powder, salt, and pepper. Toss to combine.

4. Spoon the mixture onto a rimmed baking sheet. Place the sheet in the preheated oven and roast for 20 to 25 minutes, or until the sweet potatoes are tender.

5. Serve warm or at room temperature.

• VEGAN
• PALEO
• MEDITERRANEAN

TIME-SAVING TIP:
Use pre-cut sweet potatoes and pineapple, which are sold in the produce department of most grocery stores.

ACTION PLAN TIP:
If you're using this recipe as part of the Vegan Action Plan, double the quantities so you have enough leftovers for later in the week.

PER SERVING
Calories: 230; Total Fat: 11g; Total Carbohydrates: 34g; Sugar: 5g; Fiber: 5g; Protein: 2g; Sodium: 591mg

9

Vegetarian Dishes

Quinoa-Broccolini Sauté

SERVES 4 / PREP TIME: 10 MINUTES / COOK TIME: 10 MINUTES

- VEGAN
- MEDITERRANEAN

PER SERVING
Calories: 273; Total Fat: 6g;
Total Carbohydrates: 44g;
Sugar: 5g; Fiber: 6g;
Protein: 11g; Sodium: 54mg

This recipe makes a delicious meal in a snap. Broccolini, sometimes called baby broccoli, is easy to use, and the stalks are smaller and more tender than traditional broccoli so there is less waste. Using precooked quinoa makes this a very fast meal, and you can add cooked lentils for additional protein.

1 tablespoon coconut oil

2 leeks, white part only, sliced

2 garlic cloves, chopped

4 cups chopped broccolini

½ cup vegetable broth, or water

1 teaspoon curry powder

2 cups cooked quinoa

1 tablespoon coconut aminos

1. In a large skillet over high heat, melt the coconut oil. Add the leeks and garlic. Sauté for 2 minutes.

2. Add the broccolini and vegetable broth. Cover the pan and cook for 5 minutes.

3. Stir in the curry powder, quinoa, and coconut aminos. Cook for 2 to 3 minutes, uncovered, or until the quinoa is warmed through.

4. Serve warm as a side dish, or at room temperature as a salad.

Braised Bok Choy
with Shiitake Mushrooms

SERVES 4 / PREP TIME: 10 MINUTES / COOK TIME: 10 MINUTES

Thinking of not-entirely-healthy takeout? Try this dish instead. Coconut aminos is the juice or sap from a tapped coconut tree. Here, it substitutes for soy sauce, adding depth of flavor and a touch of sweetness.

1 tablespoon coconut oil

8 baby bok choy, halved lengthwise

½ cup water

1 tablespoon coconut aminos

1 cup shiitake mushrooms, stemmed, sliced thin

Salt

Freshly ground black pepper

1 scallion, sliced thin

1 tablespoon toasted sesame seeds

1. In a large pan over high heat, melt the coconut oil. Add the bok choy in a single layer.

2. Add the water, coconut aminos, and mushrooms to the pan. Cover and braise the vegetables for 5 to 10 minutes, or until the bok choy is tender.

3. Remove the pan from the heat. Season the vegetables with salt and pepper.

4. Transfer the bok choy and mushrooms to a serving dish and garnish with the scallions and sesame seeds.

• VEGAN

• PALEO

• MEDITERRANEAN

PALEO & MEDITERRANEAN TIP:
For those on the Mediterranean and Paleo Action Plans, use chicken broth instead of water. If shiitake mushrooms are not available, or don't fit within your budget, any other type of mushroom can be used.

PER SERVING
Calories: 285; Total Fat: 8g; Total Carbohydrates: 43g; Sugar: 21g; Fiber: 18g; Protein: 26g; Sodium: 1185mg

Roasted Broccoli *and* Cashews

SERVES 4 / PREP TIME: 10 MINUTES / COOK TIME: 20 MINUTES

• VEGAN
• PALEO
• MEDITERRANEAN

Sensitivity Alert

PER SERVING
Calories: 209; Total Fat: 15g;
Total Carbohydrates: 15g;
Sugar: 3g; Fiber: 4g;
Protein: 6g; Sodium: 633mg

Roasting broccoli makes it slightly crunchy and a touch sweeter. The coconut aminos and cashews add nuttiness. This dish is great served at room temperature, making it a wonderful contribution to a potluck; it's equally delicious served warm.

6 cups broccoli florets
2 tablespoons extra-virgin
  olive oil

1 teaspoon salt
1 tablespoon coconut aminos
½ cup toasted cashews

1. Preheat the oven to 375°F.
2. In a large bowl, toss the broccoli with the olive oil and salt. Transfer the broccoli to a baking sheet, spreading it into a single layer. Place the sheet in the preheated oven and roast for 15 to 20 minutes, or until the broccoli is tender.
3. In a large bowl, toss the roasted broccoli with the coconut aminos and cashews, and serve.

Ginger Sweet Potatoes *and* Pea Hash

SERVES 4 / PREP TIME: 10 MINUTES / COOK TIME: 10 MINUTES

This hearty meal of sweet potatoes and brown rice is seasoned with an anti-inflammatory powerhouse of spices, including ginger, curry, and turmeric. Using precooked sweet potatoes and cooked brown rice makes this recipe a time-saver.

• VEGAN
• MEDITERRANEAN

Sensitivity Alert

PER SERVING
Calories: 511; Total Fat: 17g;
Total Carbohydrates: 83g;
Sugar: 4g; Fiber: 10g;
Protein: 11g; Sodium: 633mg

2 tablespoons coconut oil
4 scallions, sliced
3 garlic cloves, minced
2 teaspoons minced fresh ginger
1 teaspoon curry powder
1 teaspoon salt
½ teaspoon ground turmeric

2 medium sweet potatoes, roasted in their skins, peeled, and chopped
1 cup frozen peas
2 cups cooked brown rice
1 tablespoon coconut aminos
¼ cup chopped fresh cilantro
½ cup chopped cashews

1. In a large skillet over medium-high heat, melt the coconut oil. Add the scallions, garlic, ginger, curry powder, salt, and turmeric. Sauté for 2 minutes, or until fragrant.

2. Stir in the sweet potatoes, peas, brown rice, and coconut aminos. Sauté for 5 minutes.

3. Transfer the hash to a serving dish and garnish with the cilantro and cashews.

Buddha Bowl

SERVES 4 TO 6 / PREP TIME: 15 MINUTES / COOK TIME: 35 MINUTES

There are conflicting stories on how this dish got its name. Some say it's because it reflects Buddha's belly full of nourishment; others say it comes from Zen monks who go door to door with a bowl accepting whatever nourishment is offered. Basically, it's a bowl of rice filled with whatever vegetables you like and seasoned however you like. It's easy and stress free.

• VEGAN

• MEDITERRANEAN

INGREDIENT TIP: This recipe calls for brown basmati rice because it cooks faster but any variety of brown rice will work. If you're concerned the rice will boil over while it cooks, leave the cover slightly ajar.

1 cup brown basmati rice

2 cups vegetable broth

3 tablespoons coconut oil, divided

2 teaspoons salt, divided

1 pint sliced mushrooms

2 garlic cloves, sliced thin

4 ounces fresh snow peas, strings removed

2 carrots, sliced thin

½ cup frozen peas, thawed

2 scallions, sliced thin

3 tablespoons chopped fresh cilantro

3 tablespoons freshly squeezed lime juice

1 tablespoon toasted sesame oil

1 tablespoon coconut aminos

½ teaspoon red pepper flakes

PER SERVING

Calories: 371; Total Fat: 15g; Total Carbohydrates: 51g; Sugar: 5g; Fiber: 4g; Protein: 9g; Sodium: 1591mg

1. In a medium saucepan over high heat, stir together the basmati rice, vegetable broth, 1 tablespoon of coconut oil, and 1 teaspoon of salt. Bring to a boil, then reduce the heat to simmer. Cover the pot and cook the rice for 25 to 35 minutes, or until tender.

2. In a large pan over high heat, melt the remaining 2 tablespoons of coconut oil. Add the mushrooms. Sauté for about 5 minutes, or until they are slightly browned. ➡

Buddha Bowl
CONTINUED

3. Add the garlic, snow peas, and carrots. Sauté for 3 minutes more. Add the thawed peas and cover the pan to warm them through.

4. Add the sautéed vegetables to the rice and stir to combine. When ready to serve, stir in the scallions, cilantro, lime juice, sesame oil, coconut aminos, red pepper flakes, and the remaining 1 teaspoon of salt.

Mushroom Risotto

SERVES 4 / PREP TIME: 15 MINUTES / COOK TIME: 20 MINUTES

If you love Italian food, this dish is for you. Risotto has the reputation of being difficult to make, but, really, it is not. The secret is to add the liquid slowly while constantly stirring the rice. Once all the liquid is incorporated and the rice is tender you will have a warm, creamy, satisfying meal. If you can't find arborio rice, use any short-grain white rice. Brown rice won't work well for risotto because of its harder outer shell.

- VEGAN
- MEDITERRANEAN

COOKING TIP: If the rice isn't cooked through and you've used all the broth, add more liquid (broth or water), ¼ cup at a time, until the rice is tender. If the rice is just a touch underdone, cover the risotto, turn off the heat, and let it sit for 5 minutes.

ACTION PLAN TIP: If you're using this recipe as part of the Vegan or Mediterranean Action Plan, double the quantities so you have enough leftovers for later in the week.

2 tablespoons extra-virgin olive oil

1 large shallot, sliced

1 garlic clove, minced

1 pint sliced mushrooms

1½ cups arborio rice

3 cups vegetable broth, warmed

1 teaspoon salt

½ teaspoon freshly ground black pepper

Pinch ground nutmeg

1 tablespoon chopped fresh thyme leaves

Balsamic vinegar, for garnish

1. In a large skillet over high heat, heat the olive oil. Add the shallot and garlic. Sauté for 3 minutes.

2. Add the mushrooms and rice. Sauté for 3 minutes more.

3. Reduce the heat to medium-high. Add the vegetable broth one cup at a time, stirring constantly until the rice has absorbed the liquid before adding another cup of broth.

4. Once all the broth is absorbed add the salt, pepper, and nutmeg. Taste the risotto to see if the rice is cooked through; it should be tender but not mushy.

5. Transfer the risotto to a serving dish. Garnish with the thyme leaves and drizzle with the balsamic vinegar.

PER SERVING
Calories: 359; Total Fat: 9g; Total Carbohydrates: 60g; Sugar: 1g; Fiber: 3g; Protein: 10g; Sodium: 1162mg

Butternut Squash *and* Spinach Gratin *with* Lentils

SERVES 4 TO 6 / PREP TIME: 15 MINUTES / COOK TIME: 20 MINUTES

- VEGAN
- PALEO
- MEDITERRANEAN

Sensitivity Alert

PALEO TIP: Omit the lentils and use chicken broth instead of vegetable broth.

TIME-SAVING TIP: Use pre-cut butternut squash from the produce section of your grocery store.

ACTION PLAN TIP: If you're using this recipe as part of the Vegan Action Plan, double the quantities so you have enough leftovers for later in the week.

PER SERVING

Calories: 502; Total Fat: 37g; Total Carbohydrates: 47g; Sugar: 9g; Fiber: 16g; Protein: 20g; Sodium: 1163mg

This is a one-skillet supper, made creamy with the addition of coconut milk, and comforting with the addition of sage and walnuts. This is an easy recipe to double and freeze in single-serving containers for future meals or to take for lunch.

1 tablespoon coconut oil

1 onion, peeled and chopped

2 garlic cloves, minced

1 small butternut squash, peeled, seeded, and cut into ½-inch cubes

4 cups packed spinach

1 teaspoon salt

½ teaspoon freshly ground black pepper

1 (13.5-ounce) can coconut milk

1½ or 2 cups vegetable broth

1 (15-ounce) can lentils, drained and rinsed

¼ cup chopped fresh parsley

2 tablespoons chopped fresh sage

½ cup chopped toasted walnuts

1. Preheat the oven to 375°F.

2. In a large ovenproof skillet over high heat, melt the coconut oil. Add the onion and garlic. Sauté for 3 minutes.

3. Add the butternut squash, spinach, salt, and pepper. Sauté for 3 minutes more.

4. Stir in the coconut milk and just enough vegetable broth to cover the squash. Bring the liquid to a boil.

5. Add the lentils, parsley, and sage. Stir to combine.

6. Place the skillet in the preheated oven and bake the casserole for 15 to 20 minutes, or until the squash is tender.

7. Transfer the casserole to a serving dish and garnish with the walnuts.

Buckwheat Noodle Pad Thai

SERVES 4 / PREP TIME: 15 MINUTES / COOK TIME: 15 MINUTES

Traditional Pad Thai has tofu, peanuts, and sugar in it. The more nutritious buckwheat soba noodles replace the rice noodles in this recipe, almonds or cashews replace the peanuts, and raw honey or coconut sugar adds a touch of sweetness.

1 (8-ounce) package buckwheat soba noodles

1 tablespoon coconut oil

1 red onion, chopped

2 garlic cloves, minced

2 teaspoons minced fresh ginger

1 zucchini, chopped

2 bok choy, sliced thin

1 tablespoon coconut aminos

1 tablespoon apple cider vinegar

3 tablespoons almond butter or cashew butter

2 tablespoons toasted sesame oil

1 tablespoon raw honey or coconut sugar

¼ cup vegetable broth, or water

Salt

2 scallions, sliced thin

¼ cup chopped fresh cilantro

2 tablespoons sesame seeds

1. Cook the soba noodles according to the package directions, drain, and set aside.

2. In a large pan over high heat, melt the coconut oil. Add the red onion, garlic, ginger, zucchini, and bok choy. Sauté for 5 minutes.

3. Add the coconut aminos, cider vinegar, almond butter, sesame oil, honey, and vegetable broth. Cook for 2 minutes, stirring constantly.

4. Add the soba noodles to the pan and sauté them, using a large spatula to scoop the mixture from the bottom of the pan to the top to combine the vegetables with the noodles. Season with salt, and transfer the Pad Thai to a serving dish. Garnish with the scallions, cilantro, and sesame seeds.

• VEGAN

• MEDITERRANEAN

Sensitivity Alert

SUBSTITUTION TIP: If you prefer the more traditional rice noodles, use them instead of the soba noodles.

VEGAN TIP: If you're following the Vegan Action Plan, use the coconut sugar instead of the honey.

MEDITERRANEAN TIP: If you're following the Mediterranean Action Plan, add 2 cups of cooked cubed chicken.

ACTION PLAN TIP: If you're following the Vegan Action Plan, double the quantities so you have enough leftovers for later in the week.

PER SERVING

Calories: 486; Total Fat: 21g; Total Carbohydrates: 63g; Sugar: 12g; Fiber: 8g; Protein: 19g; Sodium: 771mg

Zucchini Stuffed *with* White Beans *and* Olives

SERVES 4 / PREP TIME: 15 MINUTES / COOK TIME: 20 MINUTES

• VEGAN

• MEDITERRANEAN

PALEO TIP: Replace the white beans with 8 ounces of cooked ground lamb.

ACTION PLAN TIP: If you're using this recipe as part of the Vegan Action Plan, double the quantities so you have enough for leftovers for later in the week.

PER SERVING
Calories: 269; Total Fat: 12g; Total Carbohydrates: 38g; Sugar: 6g; Fiber: 10g; Protein: 13g; Sodium: 873mg

White beans are the best choice for this dish; they are soft and easy to press into the zucchini boats. If you don't have time to stuff the zucchini, slice the roasted zucchini and add it to the white beans and serve as a warm salad instead.

4 large zucchini, halved lengthwise

2 tablespoons extra-virgin olive oil, plus additional for brushing

½ teaspoon salt, plus additional for seasoning

Freshly ground black pepper

Pinch ground rosemary

1 (15-ounce) can white beans, drained and rinsed

½ cup chopped pitted green olives

2 garlic cloves, minced

1 cup coarsely chopped arugula

¼ cup chopped fresh parsley

1 tablespoon apple cider vinegar

1. Preheat the oven to 375°F.

2. Brush a rimmed baking sheet with olive oil.

3. Using a small spoon or melon baller, carefully scoop out and discard the seeds from the zucchini halves.

4. Brush the scooped-out section of each zucchini boat with olive oil and lightly season the inside of each boat with salt, pepper, and rosemary.

5. Transfer the zucchini to the prepared baking sheet, cut-side up. Place the sheet in the preheated oven and roast for 15 to 20 minutes, or until the zucchini are tender and lightly browned.

6. In a medium bowl, lightly mash the white beans with a fork.

7. Add the olives, garlic, arugula, parsley, cider vinegar, the remaining ½ teaspoon of salt, and the remaining 2 tablespoons of olive oil. Season with pepper and mix well.

8. Spoon the bean mixture into the zucchini boats and serve.

One-Pot Tomato Basil Pasta

SERVES 4 / PREP TIME: 5 MINUTES / COOK TIME: 10 MINUTES

• VEGAN
• MEDITERRANEAN
• TIME-SAVING

Sensitivity Alert

ACTION PLAN TIP:
If you're using this recipe as part of the Vegan, Mediterranean, or Time-Saving Action Plan, double the quantities so you have enough leftovers for later in the week.

VARIATION TIP: For additional protein and more complex flavors, try topping the dish with microgreens like baby alfalfa sprouts.

PER SERVING
Calories: 518; Total Fat: 11g; Total Carbohydrates: 95g; Sugar: 4g; Fiber: 6g; Protein: 10g; Sodium: 909mg

It sounds impossible, but it works! Everything goes into the pot at the same time and cooks for about 10 minutes, or until the pasta is al dente. As if by magic, out comes pasta and sauce in one pot. There are many varieties of gluten-free pasta in the markets now. Check the ingredients so you don't choose one made with corn products.

2 tablespoons extra-virgin olive oil, plus additional for drizzling
1 onion, sliced thin
2 garlic cloves, sliced thin
1 pound gluten-free penne pasta
1 (15-ounce) can chopped tomatoes
1½ teaspoons salt
¼ teaspoon freshly ground black pepper
¼ cup chopped fresh basil, plus 4 whole basil leaves
4½ cups water

1. In a large, heavy-bottomed Dutch oven over medium heat, heat 2 tablespoons of olive oil. Add the onion, and garlic. Stir to coat with the oil.

2. Add the pasta, tomatoes, salt, pepper, the 4 whole basil leaves, and water to the pot. Bring the liquid to a boil and cover the pot. Cook for 8 to 10 minutes. Check the pasta to see if it is cooked; add more water if necessary. Continue cooking until the pasta is tender.

3. Transfer the pasta to a serving bowl and garnish with the remaining ¼ cup of chopped basil and a drizzle of olive oil.

Buckwheat *and* Sweet Potatoes

SERVES 4 TO 6 / PREP TIME: 15 MINUTES / COOK TIME: 20 MINUTES

• VEGAN

• MEDITERRANEAN

TIME-SAVING TIP:
Using pre-cut sweet potatoes, often sold in the produce department of the grocery store, will cut your prep time.

INGREDIENT TIP:
Buckwheat groats may be purchased in the bulk department or the hot cereal aisle.

COOKING TIP: For a creamy dish, substitute 1 cup of coconut milk for the 1 cup of vegetable broth.

PER SERVING
Calories: 427; Total Fat: 7g; Total Carbohydrates: 69g; Sugar: 4g; Fiber: 21g; Protein: 24g; Sodium: 1755mg

This dish works well because the sweet potatoes, buckwheat, and lentils all cook in the same amount of time. The kale balances the sweetness of the sweet potatoes. This recipe makes a lot, so there will definitely be leftovers for future meals.

1 tablespoon coconut oil

2 cups cubed sweet potatoes

1 yellow onion, chopped

2 garlic cloves, minced

2 teaspoons ground cumin

½ cup buckwheat groats

1 cup lentils, rinsed

6 cups vegetable broth

1 teaspoon salt

½ teaspoon freshly ground black pepper

2 cups chopped kale, thoroughly washed and stemmed

1. In a large pot over medium-high heat, melt the coconut oil. Stir in the sweet potatoes, onion, garlic, and cumin. Sauté for 5 minutes.

2. Add the buckwheat groats, lentils, vegetable broth, salt, and pepper. Bring to a boil. Reduce the heat to simmer, and cover the pot. Cook for 15 minutes, or until the sweet potatoes, buckwheat, and lentils are tender.

3. Remove the pot from the heat. Add the kale and stir to combine. Cover the pot and let it sit for 5 minutes before serving.

Savory Zucchini Patties

SERVES 2 / PREP TIME: 15 MINUTES / COOK TIME: ABOUT 5 MINUTES PER PANCAKE

These do need a bit of prep time since the zucchini is shredded and then drains for a bit, but it's worth it because the result is so versatile. Serve for breakfast as is, or topped with a fried egg for extra protein; they're also delicious with Mint Sauce (page 218) or Green Olive Tapenade (page 260).

2 medium zucchini, shredded

1 teaspoon salt, divided

2 eggs

2 tablespoons chickpea flour

1 scallion, chopped

1 tablespoon chopped fresh mint

½ teaspoon salt

2 tablespoons extra-virgin olive oil

1. Place the shredded zucchini in a fine-mesh strainer and sprinkle it with ½ teaspoon of salt. Set aside to drain while assembling the other ingredients.

2. In a medium bowl, beat together the eggs, chickpea flour, scallion, mint, and the remaining ½ teaspoon of salt.

3. Gently squeeze the zucchini to drain as much liquid as possible before adding it to the egg mixture. Stir to mix well.

4. Place a large skillet over medium-high heat.

5. When the pan is hot, add the olive oil. Drop the zucchini mixture by spoonfuls into the pan. Gently flatten the zucchini with the back of a spatula.

6. Cook for 2 to 3 minutes, or until golden brown. Flip and cook for about 2 minutes more on the other side.

7. Serve warm or at room temperature.

· MEDITERRANEAN

VEGAN TIP: If you're following the Vegan Action Plan, use the liquid drained from the beans as a substitute for the eggs. Use 3 tablespoons of liquid for each egg. Another option is to use 1 teaspoon of ground flaxseed combined with 4 tablespoons of warm water for each egg.

PALEO TIP: If you're following the Paleo Action Plan, use coconut flour instead of chickpea flour.

ACTION PLAN TIP: If you're following the Vegan or Mediterranean Action Plan, double the quantities and store the extra patties in the freezer so you have enough leftovers during the week.

PER SERVING

Calories: 263; Total Fat: 20g; Total Carbohydrates: 16g; Sugar: 6g; Fiber: 4g; Protein: 10g; Sodium: 1830mg

Veggie Soft Tacos

SERVES 4 / PREP TIME: 10 MINUTES / COOK TIME: 10 MINUTES

• VEGAN

• MEDITERRANEAN

PER SERVING
Calories: 577; Total Fat: 16g;
Total Carbohydrates: 93g;
Sugar: 14g; Fiber: 17g;
Protein: 13g; Sodium: 937mg

This recipe is a fun way to use the Mango and Black Bean Stew (page 144), but these tacos can also be made with the Quinoa-Broccolini Sauté (page 168). When purchasing gluten-free tortillas, look for ones made without cornmeal.

Extra-virgin olive oil, for brushing

8 gluten-free, corn-free tortillas

2 cups Mango and Black Bean Stew (page 144), warm

1 cup shredded red cabbage, coarsely chopped

1 avocado, pitted and chopped

½ cup chopped pineapple

1 scallion, chopped

1 teaspoon apple cider vinegar

¼ cup chopped fresh cilantro

Salt

Freshly ground black pepper

Lime wedges, for garnish

1. Preheat the oven to 350°F.

2. Brush a baking sheet with olive oil.

3. Place the tortillas on a work surface. Top each tortilla with about ¼ cup of Mango and Black Bean Stew. Fold each tortilla over and place them on the prepared baking sheet. Lightly brush the top side of the tortillas with olive oil.

4. Place the sheet in the preheated oven and warm them for about 10 minutes.

5. While the tacos are warming, in a medium bowl, mix together the cabbage, avocado, pineapple, scallion, vinegar, and cilantro. Season with salt and pepper.

6. Stuff a portion of the cabbage mixture into the warmed tacos and serve garnished with the lime wedges.

Hummus Burgers

SERVES 4 / PREP TIME: 10 MINUTES / COOK TIME: 30 MINUTES

Garlic and tahini give these burgers their Mediterranean flavors. Serve with thick slices of vine-ripened tomatoes and you'll wonder why you haven't tried this recipe sooner. For best results, let the mixture sit for about 30 minutes; it will form more easily into patties. Cook a double batch and freeze for burgers on demand. These are great accompanied with Cucumber-Yogurt Dip (page 114) or Green Olive Tapenade (page 260).

- VEGAN
- MEDITERRANEAN

ACTION PLAN TIP:
If you're using this recipe as part of the Vegan or Mediterranean Action Plan, double the quantities and freeze the extra burgers so you have enough leftovers for later in the week.

1 tablespoon extra-virgin olive oil, plus additional for brushing

2 (15-ounce) cans garbanzo beans, drained and rinsed

¼ cup tahini

1 tablespoon freshly squeezed lemon juice

2 teaspoons lemon zest

2 garlic cloves, minced

2 tablespoons chickpea flour

4 scallions, minced

1 teaspoon salt

PER SERVING
Calories: 408; Total Fat: 18g; Total Carbohydrates: 43g; Sugar: 2g; Fiber: 12g; Protein: 19g; Sodium: 625mg

1. Preheat the oven to 375°F.

2. Brush a baking sheet with olive oil.

3. In a food processor, combine the garbanzo beans, tahini, lemon juice, lemon zest, garlic, and the remaining 1 tablespoon of olive oil. Pulse until smooth.

4. Add the chickpea flour, scallions, and salt. Pulse to combine.

5. Form the mixture into four patties and place them on the prepared baking sheet. Place the sheet in the preheated oven and bake for 30 minutes.

10

Seafood Dishes

Whitefish Curry

SERVES 4 TO 6 / PREP TIME: 15 MINUTES / COOK TIME: 15 MINUTES

• PALEO

• MEDITERRANEAN

VARIATION TIP:
Salmon works well in this recipe too; or mix things up and use half salmon and half whitefish. If you do, make sure the size and thickness of the fillets are about the same so they cook at the same rate.

PER SERVING
Calories: 553; Total Fat: 39g; Total Carbohydrates: 22g; Sugar: 7g; Fiber: 6g; Protein: 34g; Sodium: 881mg

This dish has a lovely aroma from the curry, fresh ginger, and hints of lemon. If you don't like it spicy, it's just as delicious with sweet or mild curry instead. Serve as is, or garnish with toasted almonds and coconut for a satisfying crunchy texture.

2 tablespoons coconut oil

1 onion, chopped

2 garlic cloves, minced

1 tablespoon minced fresh ginger

2 teaspoons curry powder

1 teaspoon salt

¼ teaspoon freshly ground black pepper

1 (4-inch) piece lemongrass (white part only), bruised with the back of a knife

2 cups cubed butternut squash

2 cups chopped broccoli

1 (13.5-ounce) can coconut milk

1 cup vegetable broth, or chicken broth

1 pound firm whitefish fillets

¼ cup chopped fresh cilantro

1 scallion, sliced thin

Lemon wedges, for garnish

1. In a large pot over medium-high heat, melt the coconut oil. Add the onion, garlic, ginger, curry powder, salt, and pepper. Sauté for 5 minutes.

2. Add the lemongrass, butternut squash, and broccoli. Sauté for 2 minutes more.

3. Stir in the coconut milk and vegetable broth and bring to a boil. Reduce the heat to simmer and add the fish. Cover the pot and simmer for 5 minutes, or until the fish is cooked through. Remove and discard the lemongrass.

4. Ladle the curry into a serving bowl. Garnish with the cilantro and scallion and serve with the lemon wedges.

Trout *with* Sweet-and-Sour Chard

SERVES 4 / PREP TIME: 10 MINUTES / COOK TIME: 15 MINUTES

The classic sweet-and-sour chard recipe nicely complements the mild flavors of the fresh trout. Most fish counters sell boneless trout fillets; if yours doesn't, ask them to fillet it for you. You can make this dish with any firm white fish.

4 boneless trout fillets

Salt

Freshly ground black pepper

1 tablespoon extra-virgin olive oil

1 onion, chopped

2 garlic cloves, minced

2 bunches chard, sliced

¼ cup golden raisins

1 tablespoon apple cider vinegar

½ cup vegetable broth

1. Preheat the oven to 375°F.

2. Season the trout with salt and pepper.

3. In a large ovenproof pan over medium-high heat, heat the olive oil. Add the onion and garlic. Sauté for 3 minutes; add the chard and sauté for 2 minutes more.

4. Add the raisins, cider vinegar, and broth to the pan. Layer the trout fillets on top. Cover the pan and place it in the preheated oven for about 10 minutes, or until the trout is cooked through.

• PALEO
• MEDITERRANEAN

SUBSTITUTION TIP:
If you can't find trout, substitute 20 ounces of sole fillets. They should take about the same amount of time in the oven.

PER SERVING

Calories: 231; Total Fat: 10g; Total Carbohydrates: 13g; Sugar: 7g; Fiber: 2g; Protein: 24g; Sodium: 235mg

Whitefish *with* Spice Rub

SERVES 4 / PREP TIME: 3 MINUTES / COOK TIME: 12 MINUTES

Spice rubs are good to have in your pantry; they take just moments to put together and you can keep them in an airtight container at room temperature for several months. The spice combination used here is also good for chicken, salmon, and lamb. This particular recipe is great served with Kale Pesto (page 261).

2 tablespoons Slow-Cooker Ghee (page 264), melted, divided

4 (6-ounce) whitefish fillets

1 tablespoon paprika

2 teaspoons ground cumin

2 teaspoons onion powder

2 teaspoons salt

1 teaspoon ground turmeric

½ teaspoon freshly ground black pepper

1 tablespoon coconut sugar (optional)

• PALEO
• MEDITERRANEAN
• TIME-SAVING

INGREDIENT TIP:
Coconut sugar is a low glycemic, minimally processed sugar that has a flavor similar to brown sugar. It can be omitted from the rub if you choose.

_____

PER SERVING
Calories: 364; Total Fat: 20g; Total Carbohydrates: 3g; Sugar: 1g; Fiber: 1g; Protein: 42g; Sodium: 1277mg

1. Preheat the oven to 400°F.

2. Brush a shallow baking dish with 1 tablespoon of ghee.

3. Place the fish fillets in the dish and brush them with the remaining 1 tablespoon of ghee.

4. In a small bowl, combine the paprika, cumin, onion powder, salt, turmeric, pepper, and coconut sugar (if using).

5. Use 1 tablespoon of the spice rub on the fillets, making sure the surface of the fish is covered with rub. Store the remaining rub for future use.

6. Place the baking dish in the preheated oven and bake the fish for 12 to 15 minutes, or until firm and cooked through.

Pecan-Crusted Trout

SERVES 4 / PREP TIME: 15 MINUTES / COOK TIME: 15 MINUTES

• PALEO

• MEDITERRANEAN

Sensitivity Alert

PER SERVING

Calories: 672; Total Fat: 59g;
Total Carbohydrates: 13g;
Sugar: 3g; Fiber: 9g;
Protein: 30g; Sodium: 110mg

This classic dish from the American South fits well into an anti-inflammatory eating plan. Pecans are rich in magnesium, which is known to decrease inflammation. In keeping with the Southern theme, serve this trout with roasted sweet potatoes and green beans.

Extra-virgin olive oil,
  for brushing

4 large boneless trout fillets

Salt

Freshly ground black pepper

1 cup pecans, finely ground,
  divided

1 tablespoon coconut oil,
  melted, divided

2 tablespoon chopped
  fresh thyme leaves

Lemon wedges, for garnish

1. Preheat the oven to 375°F.

2. Brush a rimmed baking sheet with olive oil.

3. Place the trout fillets on the baking sheet skin-side down. Season with salt and pepper.

4. Gently press ¼ cup of ground pecans into the flesh of each fillet.

5. Drizzle the melted coconut oil over the nuts and then sprinkle the thyme over the fillets.

6. Give each fillet another sprinkle of salt and pepper.

7. Place the sheet in the preheated oven and bake for 15 minutes, or until the fish is cooked through.

Sea Bass Baked *with* Tomatoes, Olives, *and* Capers

SERVES 4 / PREP TIME: 10 MINUTES / COOK TIME: 15 MINUTES

Tomatoes, olives, and capers are classically Mediterranean. If you can find salt-cured capers, they are wonderful in this dish; just rinse them before adding. Complete the meal with brown rice and sautéed zucchini.

- PALEO
- MEDITERRANEAN

Sensitivity Alert

SUBSTITUTION TIP: Salmon and cod also work well in this recipe.

2 tablespoons extra-virgin olive oil

4 (5-ounce) sea bass fillets

1 small onion, diced

½ cup vegetable or chicken broth

1 cup canned diced tomatoes

½ cup pitted and chopped Kalamata olives

2 tablespoons capers, drained

2 cups packed spinach

1 teaspoon salt

¼ teaspoon freshly ground black pepper

PER SERVING

Calories: 273; Total Fat: 12g; Total Carbohydrates: 5g; Sugar: 2g; Fiber: 2g; Protein: 35g; Sodium: 1038mg

1. Preheat the oven to 375°F.

2. In a baking dish, add the olive oil. Place the fish fillets in the dish, turning to coat both sides with the oil.

3. Top the fish with the onion, vegetable broth, tomatoes, olives, capers, spinach, salt, and pepper.

4. Cover the baking dish with aluminum foil and place it in the preheated oven. Bake for 15 minutes, or until the fish is cooked through.

Sole *with* Vegetables *in* Foil Packets

SERVES 4 / PREP TIME: 15 MINUTES / COOK TIME: 15 MINUTES

• PALEO

• MEDITERRANEAN

PER SERVING
Calories: 224; Total Fat: 7g;
Total Carbohydrates: 4g;
Sugar: 2g; Fiber: 1g;
Protein: 35g; Sodium: 205mg

Foil packet cooking is a trend that just keeps growing in popularity. Try this dish and you'll see why! Wrapping the fish, vegetables, and aromatics in a foil package allows everything to steam in the oven, perfuming the fish with the chives. Serve this dish with rice so that it can sop up the flavorful cooking juices.

4 (5-ounce) sole fillets
Salt
Freshly ground black pepper
1 zucchini, sliced thin, divided
1 carrot, sliced thin, divided
2 shallots, sliced thin, divided
2 tablespoons snipped fresh
  chives, divided

4 teaspoons extra-virgin olive oil,
  divided
½ cup vegetable broth,
  or water, divided
Lemon wedges, for garnish

1. Preheat the oven to 425°F.

2. Tear off four 12-by-20-inch pieces of aluminum foil.

3. Place 1 fillet on one half of a foil piece. Season with salt and pepper.

4. Top the fillet with one-quarter each of the zucchini, carrot, and shallots. Sprinkle with 1½ teaspoons of chives.

5. Drizzle 1 teaspoon of olive oil and 2 tablespoons of vegetable broth over the vegetables and fish.

6. Fold the other half of the foil over the fish and vegetables, sealing the edges so the ingredients are completely encased in the packet and the contents won't leak. Place the packet on a large baking sheet.

7. Repeat steps 3 through 6 with the remaining ingredients.

8. Place the sheet in the preheated oven and bake the packets for 15 minutes, or until the fish is cooked through and the vegetables are tender.

9. Carefully peel back the foil (the escaping steam will be hot) and transfer the contents—the liquid, too—to a plate. Serve garnished with the lemon wedges.

Salmon
with Basil Gremolata

SERVES 4 / PREP TIME: 10 MINUTES / COOK TIME: 20 MINUTES

• PALEO

• MEDITERRANEAN

RECIPE TIP: Basil
will oxidize and turn
brown quickly, so it's
best to consume the
gremolata within hours
of making it.

ACTION PLAN TIP:
If you're using this
recipe as part of the
Paleo or Mediterranean
Action Plan, double
the quantities so you
have enough leftovers
for later in the week.

PER SERVING

Calories: 274; Total Fat: 12g;
Total Carbohydrates: 11g;
Sugar: 5g; Fiber: 5g;
Protein: 32g; Sodium: 908mg

Gremolata is a simple Italian condiment made of parsley, garlic, and lemons. In this dish, basil is used instead of parsley; basil provides great flavor and flavonoids, which help repair cell structure.

4 (5-ounce) skin-on salmon fillets

1 tablespoon plus 2 teaspoons extra-virgin olive oil, divided

¼ cup freshly squeezed lemon juice

1 teaspoon salt, plus additional for seasoning

¼ teaspoon freshly ground black pepper, plus additional for seasoning

1 bunch basil

1 garlic clove

1 tablespoon lemon zest

1 (8-ounce) bag mixed greens

1 small cucumber, halved lengthwise and sliced thin

1 cup sprouts (radish, onion, or sunflower)

1. Preheat the oven to 375°F.

2. In a shallow baking dish, place the salmon fillets and brush them with 2 teaspoons of olive oil.

3. Add the lemon juice. Season with 1 teaspoon of salt and ¼ teaspoon of pepper.

4. Place the dish in the preheated oven and bake the fillets for about 20 minutes, or until firm and cooked through.

5. In a food processor, combine the basil, garlic, and lemon zest. Process until coarsely chopped.

6. Arrange the greens, cucumber, and sprouts on a serving platter. Drizzle the greens with the remaining 2 tablespoons of olive oil and season with salt and pepper. Place the salmon fillets on top of the greens and spoon the gremolata over the salmon.

Swordfish *with* Pineapple *and* Cilantro

SERVES 4 / PREP TIME: 15 MINUTES / COOK TIME: 20 MINUTES

• PALEO

• MEDITERRANEAN

SUBSTITUTION TIP:
Salmon works well in
this recipe, too.

PER SERVING
Calories: 408; Total Fat: 16g;
Total Carbohydrates: 7g;
Sugar: 4g; Fiber: 1g;
Protein: 60g; Sodium: 858mg

Pineapple and coconut aminos give this recipe a tropical flair. Everything is baked together, which means you'll have dinner in no time—and cleanup is quick too. Served alongside rice cooked in coconut milk and water and Avocado and Mango Salad (page 149), you can close your eyes and feel the breeze.

1 tablespoon coconut oil

2 pounds swordfish, or other
 firm white fish, cut into
 2-inch pieces

1 cup fresh pineapple chunks

¼ cup chopped fresh cilantro

2 tablespoons chopped
 fresh parsley

2 garlic cloves, minced

1 tablespoon coconut aminos

1 teaspoon salt

¼ teaspoon freshly ground
 black pepper

1. Preheat the oven to 400°F.

2. Grease a baking dish with the coconut oil.

3. Add the swordfish, pineapple, cilantro, parsley, garlic, coconut aminos, salt, and pepper to the dish. Gently mix the ingredients together.

4. Place the dish in the preheated oven and bake for 15 to 20 minutes, or until the fish feels firm to the touch. Serve warm.

Oven-Roasted Cod *with* Mushrooms

SERVES 4 TO 6 / PREP TIME: 10 MINUTES / COOK TIME: 20 MINUTES

Cod is a dense white fish that pairs well with the earthy flavor of shiitake mushrooms, which are a good source of iron. Their smoky flavor really adds depth to this recipe, too. Serve this dish with buckwheat soba noodles and sliced cucumbers.

- PALEO
- MEDITERRANEAN

PER SERVING

Calories: 221; Total Fat: 6g;
Total Carbohydrates: 12g;
Sugar: 3g; Fiber: 2g;
Protein: 32g; Sodium: 637mg

1½ pounds cod fillets

½ teaspoon salt, plus additional for seasoning

Freshly ground black pepper

1 tablespoon extra-virgin olive oil

1 leek, white part only, sliced thin

8 ounces shiitake mushrooms, stemmed, sliced

1 tablespoon coconut aminos

1 teaspoon sweet paprika

½ cup vegetable broth, or chicken broth

1. Preheat the oven to 375°F.

2. Season the cod with salt and pepper. Set aside.

3. In a shallow baking dish, combine the olive oil, leek, mushrooms, coconut aminos, paprika, and ½ teaspoon of salt. Season with pepper, and give everything a gentle toss to coat with the oil and spices.

4. Place the dish in the preheated oven and bake the vegetables for 10 minutes.

5. Stir the vegetables and place the cod fillets on top in a single layer.

6. Pour in the vegetable broth. Return the dish to the oven and bake for an additional 10 to 15 minutes, or until the cod is firm but cooked through.

Cod *with* Lentils *and* Vegetables

SERVES 4 / PREP TIME: 15 MINUTES / COOK TIME: 20 MINUTES

· ·

· MEDITERRANEAN

SUBSTITUTION TIP:
Extra-virgin olive oil can replace ghee in this recipe.

ACTION PLAN TIP:
If you're using this recipe as part of the Mediterranean Action Plan, double the quantities so you have enough leftovers for later in the week.

PER SERVING
Calories: 450; Total Fat: 6g;
Total Carbohydrates: 51g;
Sugar: 7g; Fiber: 19g;
Protein: 51g; Sodium: 1251mg

Pan-fried fish and lentils is a classic French dish. Here, it's simplified by using canned lentils, and the cod is seared only briefly in the pan before finishing in the oven. Leftovers can be eaten cold or at room temperature.

Cooking spray

1 tablespoon Slow-Cooker Ghee (page 264)

4 (6-ounce) cod fillets

1 teaspoon salt

¼ teaspoon freshly ground black pepper

2 shallots, sliced thin

1 garlic clove, sliced thin

2 carrots, diced

1 medium turnip, diced

2 cups shredded kale, thoroughly washed

2 (15-ounce) cans lentils, drained and rinsed

1 tablespoon apple cider vinegar

1. Preheat the oven to 375°F.

2. Lightly coat a rimmed baking sheet with cooking spray.

3. In a large pan over high heat, melt the ghee.

4. While the ghee is melting, sprinkle the cod with the salt and the pepper. Place each fillet top-side down in the pan (the top side is the plumper, rounded side of the fillet).

5. Sear the fillets for about 4 minutes, or until golden.

6. Transfer the fillets to the prepared baking sheet, top-side up. Place the sheet in the preheated oven and bake for 15 to 20 minutes, or until firm and cooked through.

7.   While the fish is baking, add the shallots and garlic to the pan used to sear the fish. Sauté for 3 minutes.

8.   Add the carrots and turnip. Sauté for 10 minutes more, or until tender.

9.   Add the kale, lentils, and cider vinegar to the pan and cook for about 1 minute to warm through. Remove the pan from the heat.

10.   Divide the lentil mixture among four plates and top each with a cod fillet.

Sesame-Tuna Skewers

SERVES 4 TO 6 / PREP TIME: 20 MINUTES/ COOK TIME: 15 MINUTES

Fresh tuna is coated in sesame seeds and spices and baked on skewers for easy eating. Serve with shaved cucumbers, radishes, and Chicken Lettuce Wraps sauce (page 212). Salmon or swordfish can replace tuna if it's not available or out of your budget.

- PALEO
- MEDITERRANEAN

COOKING TIP: The cooking time given is for very rare tuna. If you like your tuna cooked more, remove it from the oven at 10 minutes, cover the skewers with aluminum foil so the sesame seeds don't burn, and bake for an additional 5 minutes.

Cooking spray

¾ cup sesame seeds
  (mixture of black and white)

1 teaspoon salt

½ teaspoon ground ginger

¼ teaspoon freshly ground black pepper

2 tablespoons toasted sesame oil, or extra-virgin olive oil

4 (6-ounce) thick tuna steaks, cut into 1-inch cubes

1. Preheat the oven to 400°F.
2. Lightly coat a rimmed baking sheet with cooking spray.
3. Soak 12 (6-inch) wooden skewers in water so they won't burn while the tuna bakes.
4. In a shallow dish, combine the sesame seeds, salt, ground ginger, and pepper.
5. In a medium bowl, toss the tuna with the sesame oil to coat. Press the oiled cubes into the sesame seed mixture. Put three cubes on each skewer.
6. Place the skewers on the prepared baking sheet and place the sheet into the preheated oven. Bake for 10 to 12 minutes, turning once halfway through.

PER SERVING

Calories: 395; Total Fat: 22g; Total Carbohydrates: 7g; Sugar: 0g; Fiber: 3g; Protein: 45g; Sodium: 649mg

Mediterranean Fish Stew

SERVES 4 / PREP TIME: 15 MINUTES / COOK TIME: 15 MINUTES

....

This is a classic dish originally made by fishermen to use up any fish they couldn't sell. Any firm-fleshed fish will do and you can make it with salmon if you don't care for white fish. If you're lucky enough to have leftovers, they need to be eaten within several days. Sadly, fish dishes don't freeze well.

1 tablespoon extra-virgin olive oil, plus additional as needed

1 white onion, sliced thin

1 fennel bulb, sliced thin

2 garlic cloves, minced

1 (28-ounce) can crushed tomatoes

Pinch saffron threads

1 teaspoon ground cumin

1 teaspoon ground oregano

1 teaspoon salt

½ teaspoon freshly ground black pepper

2 pounds firm white fish fillets, cut into 2-inch pieces

2 tablespoons chopped fresh parsley

½ lemon, for garnish

1. In a large pot or pan over medium-high heat, heat 1 tablespoon of olive oil. Add the onion, fennel, and garlic. Sauté for 5 minutes.

2. Stir in the crushed tomatoes, saffron threads, cumin, oregano, salt, and pepper. Bring the mixture to a simmer.

3. Lay the fish fillets in a single layer over the vegetables, cover the pan, and simmer for 10 minutes.

4. Transfer the fish and vegetables to a serving platter. Garnish with the parsley, a drizzle of olive oil, and a generous squeeze of lemon juice.

Salmon Baked
with Leeks *and* Fennel

SERVES 4 / PREP TIME: 10 MINUTES / COOK TIME: 20 MINUTES

* * * * * * *

Salmon is loaded with healthy fats, and leeks and fennel aid digestion. As the dish bakes, the rosemary infuses everything with its distinctive flavor. Need the perfect accompaniment? Roasted sweet potatoes and sautéed spinach will do the trick.

1 tablespoon extra-virgin olive oil, plus additional for brushing

1 leek, white part only, sliced thin

1 fennel bulb, sliced thin

4 (5- to 6-ounce) salmon fillets

1 teaspoon salt

¼ teaspoon freshly ground black pepper

½ cup vegetable broth, or water

1 fresh rosemary sprig

1. Preheat the oven to 375°F.

2. In a shallow roasting pan, add 1 tablespoon of olive oil. Add the leek and fennel. Stir to coat with the oil.

3. Place the salmon fillets over the vegetables and sprinkle with salt and pepper.

4. Pour in the vegetable broth and add the rosemary sprig to the pan. Cover tightly with aluminum foil.

5. Place the pan in the preheated oven and bake for 20 minutes, or until the salmon is cooked through.

6. Remove and discard the rosemary sprig. Transfer the salmon and vegetables to a platter and serve.

• PALEO

• MEDITERRANEAN

RECIPE TIP: Leftovers can be added to a salad for lunch.

ACTION PLAN TIP: If you're using this recipe as part of the Mediterranean Action Plan, double the quantities so you have enough leftovers for later in the week.

PER SERVING

Calories: 288; Total Fat: 14g; Total Carbohydrates: 8g; Sugar: 1g; Fiber: 2g; Protein: 34g; Sodium: 692mg

Baked Spice Salmon Steaks

SERVES 4 / PREP TIME: 5 MINUTES / COOK TIME: 15 TO 20 MINUTES

· ·

- PALEO
- MEDITERRANEAN

RECIPE TIP: To make roasted asparagus, wash and dry one bunch of asparagus and remove the tough bottom inch of the stems. Drizzle the asparagus with 1 teaspoon of extra-virgin olive oil and season with ½ teaspoon of salt. Place on an aluminum foil-lined baking sheet. Roast at 375°F for 10 to 15 minutes, or until tender.

PER SERVING

Calories: 255; Total Fat: 14g; Total Carbohydrates: 0g; Sugar: 0g; Fiber: 0g; Protein: 33g; Sodium: 210mg

Salmon steaks have bones in and skin on, which makes them very moist and tender. The same spice rub mix used for Whitefish with Spice Rub (page 191) is used here. Since the oven is on to bake the salmon, throw in a bunch of asparagus to roast, rounding out the meal.

Cooking spray

4 (6-ounce) salmon steaks

1 tablespoon extra-virgin olive oil

1 tablespoon Spice Rub (page 191)

1. Preheat the oven to 375°F.

2. Lightly spray a rimmed baking sheet with cooking spray.

3. Place the salmon steaks on the baking sheet and brush both sides with olive oil.

4. Season both sides of the steaks with the spice rub.

5. Place the sheet in the preheated oven and bake the salmon for 15 to 20 minutes, or until the steaks are firm and cooked through.

Salmon *with* Quinoa

SERVES 4 / PREP TIME: 10 MINUTES / COOK TIME: 20 MINUTES

Sensitivity Alert

PALEO TIP: Omit the quinoa and serve the baked salmon with the sautéed vegetables spooned over the fillets.

PER SERVING
Calories: 396; Total Fat: 16g;
Total Carbohydrates: 36g;
Sugar: 4g; Fiber: 6g;
Protein: 30g; Sodium: 395mg

Tomatoes, basil, and green olives give this recipe its robust flavor—one that is quintessentially Mediterranean. This dish is good served warm or at room temperature. Leftovers can be tossed with greens and served as a salad.

1 tablespoon extra-virgin olive oil, plus additional for brushing
1 pound salmon fillets
Salt
Freshly ground black pepper
1 red onion, diced

2 cups cooked quinoa
1 pint cherry tomatoes, halved
½ cup chopped fresh basil
¼ cup chopped green olives
1 tablespoon apple cider vinegar

1. Preheat the oven to 375°F.

2. Brush a rimmed baking sheet with olive oil. Place the salmon fillets on the prepared sheet and brush the top of each with olive oil. Season with salt and pepper.

3. Place the sheet in the preheated oven and bake for 20 minutes.

4. In a large pan over medium-high heat, heat 1 tablespoon of olive oil. Add the onion and sauté for 3 minutes.

5. Stir in the quinoa, cherry tomatoes, basil, olives, and cider vinegar. Cook for 1 to 2 minutes, or until the tomatoes and quinoa are warmed through.

6. Transfer the tomatoes, quinoa, and salmon to a serving platter and serve.

Salmon Cakes
with Mango Salsa

SERVES 4 / PREP TIME: 15 MINUTES / COOK TIME: 20 MINUTES

These salmon cakes are oven-baked, so there's no smelly frying mess. Serve on a bed of lightly dressed greens with sliced avocado. Make a double batch and freeze the extras to reheat another time.

2 tablespoons coconut oil, melted, divided

1 egg

2 teaspoons Dijon mustard

1 teaspoon Worcestershire sauce

Dash hot sauce

2 scallions, sliced

1 ½ pounds salmon fillets, cut into 1-inch pieces

1 teaspoon salt

¼ teaspoon freshly ground white pepper

1 recipe Mango Salsa (page 157)

1. Preheat the oven to 400°F.

2. Brush a rimmed baking sheet with 1 tablespoon of melted coconut oil.

3. In a food processor, combine the egg, Dijon mustard, Worcestershire sauce, hot sauce, scallions, salmon, salt, and white pepper. Pulse the ingredients until the salmon is finely chopped and the resulting mixture can be shaped into patties.

4. Shape the mixture into four large patties of equal size.

5. Place the patties on the prepared baking sheet and brush them with the remaining 1 tablespoon of melted coconut oil.

6. Place the sheet in the preheated oven and bake for 15 to 20 minutes, or until lightly browned and firm to the touch.

7. Serve warm with Mango Salsa.

• PALEO
• MEDITERRANEAN

RECIPE TIP: Add two ounces of smoked salmon to a food processor with the other ingredients to give these cakes a smoky flavor.

SUBSTITUTION TIP: You can use a firm-fleshed white fish like cod or halibut in this recipe in place of the salmon.

ACTION PLAN TIP: If you're following the Mediterranean Action Plan, double the amounts and freeze the leftovers so you'll have enough later in the week.

PER SERVING

Calories: 385; Total Fat: 19g; Total Carbohydrates: 20g; Sugar: 17g; Fiber: 3g; Protein: 35g; Sodium: 762mg

11

Meat & Poultry Dishes

Chicken Lettuce Wraps

SERVES 4 / PREP TIME: 20 MINUTES

• PALEO

• MEDITERRANEAN

STORAGE TIP: The dressing can be made up to a week ahead and stored in an airtight container in the refrigerator.

PER SERVING

Calories: 342; Total Fat: 30g; Total Carbohydrates: 13g; Sugar: 4g; Fiber: 3g; Protein: 7g; Sodium: 40mg

Inspired by the lettuce cups served in many restaurants, this version is a fun and tasty meal for the whole family. Having the ingredients prepped and on hand makes this a fast dinner on a busy night.

2 heads butter lettuce, 8 lettuce cups total

1 pound grilled boneless skin-on chicken breast, cut into ½-inch cubes

1 cup shredded carrots

½ cup thinly sliced radishes

2 scallions, sliced thin

2 tablespoons chopped fresh cilantro

½ cup toasted sesame oil

3 tablespoons freshly squeezed lime juice

1 tablespoon coconut aminos

1 garlic clove

1 thin slice fresh ginger

1 teaspoon lime zest

1 tablespoon sesame seeds, divided

1. Place the lettuce cups on a serving platter.

2. Evenly divide the chicken, carrots, radishes, scallions, and cilantro among the lettuce cups.

3. In a blender or food processor, combine the sesame oil, lime juice, coconut aminos, garlic, ginger, and lime zest. Blend until smooth.

4. Drizzle the chicken and vegetables with the dressing and sprinkle each with sesame seeds.

Chicken Breast
with Cherry Sauce

SERVES 4 / PREP TIME: 10 MINUTES / COOK TIME: 30 MINUTES

. . . .

Cherries are loaded with anti-inflammatory properties and are said to help with gout and other joint-related issues. The coconut oil used here enhances the fruitiness of the dried cherries and the balsamic vinegar adds depth. Serve with Cauliflower Purée (page 163) and steamed broccoli to make a complete meal.

1 tablespoon coconut oil

4 boneless skinless chicken breasts

Salt

Freshly ground black pepper

2 scallions, sliced

¾ cup chicken broth

1 tablespoon balsamic vinegar

½ cup dried cherries

- PALEO
- MEDITERRANEAN

PER SERVING

Calories: 379; Total Fat: 14g;
Total Carbohydrates: 17g;
Sugar: 9g; Fiber: 5g;
Protein: 43g; Sodium: 308mg

1. Preheat the oven to 375°F.

2. In a large ovenproof skillet over medium-high heat, melt the coconut oil.

3. Season the chicken with salt and pepper. Place the chicken in the pan and brown it on both sides, about 3 minutes per side.

4. Add the scallions, chicken broth, balsamic vinegar, and dried cherries. Cover with an ovenproof lid or aluminum foil and place the pan in the preheated oven. Bake for 20 minutes, or until the chicken is cooked through.

Chicken *with* Fennel *and* Zucchini

SERVES 4 / PREP TIME: 15 MINUTES / COOK TIME: 15 MINUTES

• PALEO

• MEDITERRANEAN

TIME-SAVING TIP:
Many large grocery stores sell pre-cut chicken breast strips in the self-serve section.

PER SERVING
Calories: 418; Total Fat: 20g; Total Carbohydrates: 15g; Sugar: 5g; Fiber: 4g; Protein: 45g; Sodium: 1121mg

A Mediterranean stir-fry! By cutting the breast meat into strips, it cooks in no time. If your chicken is frozen, defrost it about halfway and then cut it into the strips. It's easier to cut when still partially frozen. Plus, it'll finish defrosting by about the time it's ready to go in the pan.

2 tablespoons extra-virgin olive oil

4 boneless skinless chicken breasts, cut into strips

1 leek, white part only, sliced thin

1 fennel bulb, sliced into ¼-inch rounds

3 zucchini, sliced into ½-inch rounds

½ cup chicken broth

1 teaspoon salt

½ teaspoon freshly ground black pepper

½ cup sliced green olives

2 tablespoons chopped fresh dill

1. In a large pan over high heat, heat the olive oil.

2. Add the chicken strips. Brown them for 1 to 2 minutes, stirring constantly. Transfer the chicken and its juices to a plate or bowl and set aside.

3. Add the leek, fennel, and zucchini to the pan. Sauté for 5 minutes.

4. Return the chicken and juices to the pan. Pour in the broth. Add the salt and pepper. Cover the pan and simmer for 5 minutes.

5. Remove the pan from the heat, and stir in the olives and dill.

Sesame, Broccoli, Carrot, *and* Chicken Stir-Fry

SERVES 4 TO 6 / PREP TIME: 15 MINUTES / COOK TIME: 15 MINUTES

A stir-fry is the ultimate one-pot meal. Since this one is so easy to make, it's worth making a double batch. You'll be happy with these leftovers, whether for lunch or another dinner.

- PALEO
- MEDITERRANEAN

PER SERVING
Calories: 305; Total Fat: 14g;
Total Carbohydrates: 8g;
Sugar: 2g; Fiber: 2g;
Protein: 35g; Sodium: 812mg

1 pound boneless skinless chicken thighs, cut into thin strips
1 tablespoon coconut oil
2 cups broccoli florets
2 carrots, cut into matchsticks
1 garlic clove, minced
1 teaspoon minced fresh ginger

1 teaspoon salt
¼ teaspoon red pepper flakes
½ cup chicken broth
1 teaspoon toasted sesame oil
1 teaspoon coconut aminos
1 tablespoon sesame seeds

1. In a large pan or Dutch oven over high heat, melt the coconut oil. Add the chicken and sauté for 5 to 8 minutes, or until the chicken browns.

2. Stir in the broccoli, carrots, garlic, ginger, salt, red pepper flakes, and chicken broth. Cover the pan and cook for 5 minutes, or until the broccoli turns bright green.

3. Remove the pan from the heat and stir in the sesame oil, coconut aminos, and sesame seeds.

Chicken *with* Brown Rice *and* Snow Peas

SERVES 4 / PREP TIME: 10 MINUTES / COOK TIME: 5 MINUTES

This is a great use of leftover rice and chicken. Snow peas have vitamin C and magnesium, and are kid-friendly. They have a crispy texture and a slightly sweet flavor.

- MEDITERRANEAN
- TIME-SAVING

PER SERVING
Calories: 285; Total Fat: 7g;
Total Carbohydrates: 39g;
Sugar: 1g; Fiber: 3g;
Protein: 15g; Sodium: 705mg

1 tablespoon coconut oil

2 cups cooked brown rice

1 cup cooked chicken, cut into ½-inch cubes

4 ounces snow peas, strings removed

½ cup chicken broth

1 teaspoon salt

½ teaspoon ground ginger

1 teaspoon toasted sesame oil

1 teaspoon coconut aminos

2 scallions, sliced

1. In a large pan over high heat, melt the coconut oil. Add the rice and chicken. Sauté for about 2 minutes.

2. Add the snow peas, chicken broth, salt, and ginger. Cover the pan, reduce the heat to low, and cook for 3 minutes, or until the snow peas turn bright green.

3. Remove the pan from the heat. Stir in the sesame oil, coconut aminos, and scallions.

Chicken Skewers *with* Mint Sauce

SERVES 4 TO 6 / PREP TIME: 20 MINUTES / COOK TIME: 20 MINUTES

- PALEO
- MEDITERRANEAN

COOKING TIP: If you are concerned about cooking the chicken thoroughly, grill the skewers first to get the grill marks and then finish them in a 375°F oven for 10 minutes.

PER SERVING

Calories: 657; Total Fat: 51g; Total Carbohydrates: 2g; Sugar: 0g; Fiber: 1g; Protein: 50g; Sodium: 1024mg

These make a great dinner or appetizer. Make them for your next party and watch them disappear. You can prepare the chicken the night before and skewer them right before grilling. The mint sauce can be made a few days ahead.

FOR THE MINT SAUCE

1 bunch fresh mint, stemmed
½ cup extra-virgin olive oil
1 garlic clove
2 teaspoons lemon zest
½ teaspoon salt
Pinch freshly ground black pepper

FOR THE CHICKEN

6 boneless skinless chicken breasts, cut into 1½- to 2-inch cubes
¼ cup extra-virgin olive oil
¼ cup freshly squeezed lemon juice
1 teaspoon salt
¼ teaspoon freshly ground black pepper
Pinch ground turmeric
2 fresh mint sprigs

To make the mint sauce

1. In a blender or food processor, combine the mint, olive oil, garlic, lemon zest, salt, and pepper. Blend until smooth.

2. Refrigerate in an airtight container for no more than four or five days.

To make the chicken

1. Soak 12 (6-inch) wooden skewers in water for at least 30 minutes so the skewers won't burn while on the grill.

2. In a large zip-top plastic bag, combine the chicken, olive oil, lemon juice, salt, pepper, turmeric, and mint. Close the bag, refrigerate, turn to coat, and let marinate at least 30 minutes, or overnight.

3. Preheat the grill, or place a stovetop grill over high heat.

4. Put 3 or 4 chicken cubes on each skewer. Discard the marinade and mint sprigs.

5. Reduce the grill to medium. Grill the chicken for 15 to 20 minutes, turning occasionally, until each skewer is marked on both sides and the chicken is cooked through.

6. Serve with the mint sauce.

Southwest Chicken *and* Black Bean Rice Bowl

SERVES 4 / PREP TIME: 20 MINUTES / COOK TIME: 35 MINUTES

• MEDITERRANEAN

PER SERVING
Calories: 623; Total Fat: 19g;
Total Carbohydrates: 60g;
Sugar: 3g; Fiber: 7g;
Protein: 52g; Sodium: 1092mg

This is an inside-out burrito; all that's missing is the tortilla. The chicken breast is rubbed with a mixture of chipotle and cumin and served over brown rice, butternut squash, and black beans. Serve with lime wedges for a true Southwestern flavor.

4 boneless skinless chicken breasts

1 teaspoon salt

½ teaspoon chipotle powder

½ teaspoon ground cumin

2 tablespoons extra-virgin olive oil

1 onion, chopped

1 cup brown basmati rice

2 cups butternut squash, cut into ½-inch pieces

2 cups chicken broth

1 cup cooked black beans

1 lime, cut into 8 wedges

1. Place the chicken on a large plate.

2. In a small bowl, mix together the salt, chipotle powder, and cumin. Rub the mixture onto the chicken breasts.

3. Place a large pan or Dutch oven over high heat and add the olive oil. When the oil is hot, add the chicken and brown it, about 3 minutes per side. Remove the chicken from the pan and transfer it to a plate.

4. Add the onions to the pan. Sauté for about 3 minutes, or until just softened.

5. Stir in the rice, butternut squash, and chicken broth.

6. Return the chicken to the pan and cover it. Bring to a boil, reduce the heat to simmer, and cook for 20 minutes.

7. Remove the pan from the heat and stir in the black beans. Serve with the lime wedges.

Spice-Rubbed Chicken

SERVES 4 TO 6 / PREP TIME: 10 MINUTES / COOK TIME: 45 MINUTES

- PALEO
- MEDITERRANEAN

ACTION PLAN TIP:
If you're using this recipe as part of the Paleo Action Plan, double the quantities so you have enough leftovers for later in the week.

PER SERVING
Calories: 375; Total Fat: 21g; Total Carbohydrates: 10g; Sugar: 7g; Fiber: 1g; Protein: 39g; Sodium: 1030mg

Almost nothing beats home-cooked chicken . . . the comforting smell alone is worth the effort. The brown rice flour (or coconut flour if you're Paleo) helps give the chicken skin a crunchy texture, and the spices are the classic blend used by most markets for making rotisserie chicken. By cutting the chicken into pieces, the cooking time is cut significantly. Apple juice keeps it all moist. Since the oven is already on to cook the chicken, make some roasted vegetables and sweet potatoes to round out your meal.

1 whole chicken, cut into 8 pieces

1 tablespoon brown rice flour, or coconut flour

1 teaspoon salt

1 teaspoon ground cumin

2 teaspoons sweet paprika

½ teaspoon garlic powder

½ teaspoon freshly ground black pepper

1 cup no-added-sugar apple juice

1. Preheat the oven to 375°F.

2. Place the chicken pieces in a baking pan.

3. In a small bowl, combine the brown rice flour, salt, cumin, paprika, garlic powder, and pepper. Rub the spice mix onto the chicken pieces.

4. Carefully pour the apple juice into the pan; avoid washing the spice mixture off the chicken.

5. Place the pan in the preheated oven and bake for 35 to 45 minutes, or until the chicken is golden brown and cooked through.

Chicken Thighs *with* Sweet Potatoes

SERVES 4 TO 6 / PREP TIME: 10 MINUTES / COOK TIME: 45 MINUTES

Chicken thighs are almost impossible to overcook. The dark meat and bone keep them moist. If the thighs are on the small side, they will cook in about 35 minutes. The sweet potatoes contribute sugar, which helps brown the chicken, and they absorb all the deliciousness of the roasting juices and spices. Add a fresh garden salad or Green Beans with Crispy Shallots (page 164) for dinner.

2 tablespoons extra-virgin olive oil or coconut oil

2 shallots, sliced thin

1 teaspoon salt

½ teaspoon ground cumin

½ teaspoon ground cinnamon

¼ teaspoon freshly ground black pepper

1 cup chicken broth

6 bone-in chicken thighs

2 small sweet potatoes, peeled and cut into ½-inch cubes

1. Preheat the oven to 425°F.

2. In a large baking dish, stir together the oil, shallots, salt, cumin, cinnamon, pepper, and chicken broth.

3. Add the chicken and sweet potatoes. Stir to coat with the spices.

4. Place the dish in the preheated oven and bake for 35 to 45 minutes, or until the chicken is cooked through and the sweet potatoes are tender.

- PALEO
- MEDITERRANEAN

ACTION PLAN TIP:
If you're using this recipe as part of the Paleo or Mediterranean Action Plan, double the quantities so you have enough leftovers for later in the week.

PER SERVING
Calories: 524; Total Fat: 33g; Total Carbohydrates: 22g; Sugar: 1g; Fiber: 3g; Protein: 33g; Sodium: 908mg

Chicken Curry

SERVES 4 TO 6 / PREP TIME: 10 MINUTES / COOK TIME: 4 HOURS

A classic curry begins with sautéing the aromatic vegetables in ghee. Ghee is butter that has been slowly cooked and strained of its solids, leaving behind a pure buttery oil. Even though ghee is made from dairy, once processed most people with dairy intolerances can digest it. Since this curry is made in the slow cooker, the sautéing step is skipped.

1 tablespoon Slow-Cooker Ghee (page 264)

3 pounds boneless skinless chicken thighs

2 onions, chopped

2 garlic cloves, sliced thin

2 teaspoons minced fresh ginger

1 tablespoon curry powder

1 teaspoon ground coriander

1 teaspoon ground cumin

1 teaspoon salt

2 cups chicken broth

1 cup coconut milk

¼ cup fresh cilantro leaves

- PALEO
- MEDITERRANEAN
- TIME-SAVING

SUBSTITUTION TIP: If you don't have ghee, use an equal amount of coconut oil or extra-virgin olive oil.

VARIATION TIP: For a different taste that is still complementary, try swapping the cilantro with Thai basil.

PER SERVING
Calories: 866; Total Fat: 43g; Total Carbohydrates: 11g; Sugar: 5g; Fiber: 3g; Protein: 103g; Sodium: 1270mg

1. In the slow cooker, combine the ghee, chicken, onions, garlic, ginger, curry powder, coriander, cumin, salt, chicken broth, and coconut milk. Cover and cook on high for 4 hours.

2. Just before serving, stir in the cilantro.

Coconut Chicken

SERVES 4 TO 6 / PREP TIME: 10 MINUTES / COOK TIME: 6 HOURS

· PALEO

· MEDITERRANEAN

· TIME-SAVING

ACTION PLAN TIP:
If you're using this recipe as part of the Paleo, Mediterranean, or Time-Saving Action Plan, double the quantities so you have enough leftovers for later in the week.

PER SERVING
Calories: 652; Total Fat: 56g;
Total Carbohydrates: 10g;
Sugar: 5g; Fiber: 3g;
Protein: 32g; Sodium: 1277mg

While delicious all on its own, this recipe can be made even heartier by adding 2 cups of cubed sweet potatoes or winter squash and 1 pint of whole mushrooms (stemmed). Serve with rice or mashed sweet potatoes.

1 tablespoon coconut oil
6 bone-in skin-on chicken thighs
1 onion, sliced
2 garlic cloves, smashed
2 teaspoons curry powder
1 teaspoon salt
¼ teaspoon freshly ground black pepper
1 (13.5-ounce) can coconut milk
3 cups chicken broth
¼ cup chopped fresh cilantro
2 scallions, sliced

1. Coat the slow cooker with the coconut oil.

2. Add the chicken, onion, garlic, curry powder, salt, pepper, coconut milk, and chicken broth. Cover the slow cooker and cook on high for 6 hours.

3. Garnish with the cilantro and scallions before serving.

Chicken Fingers *with* Honey-Mustard-Sesame Sauce

SERVES 4 / PREP TIME: 20 MINUTES / COOK TIME: 15 MINUTES

Chicken fingers are a big hit with kids, and making them yourself provides a healthy option for your family. They are also a great appetizer for entertaining. Make a double batch and freeze them in a single layer. Reheat a few in the toaster oven for a quick snack.

2 tablespoons coconut oil, melted

4 boneless skinless chicken breasts, cut into strips

1 cup coconut milk

1½ cups rice or coconut flour

1 teaspoon salt

1 teaspoon onion powder

½ teaspoon paprika

½ teaspoon mustard powder

¼ teaspoon garlic powder

1 recipe Honey-Mustard-Sesame Sauce (page 262)

1. Preheat the oven to 400°F.

2. Coat a rimmed baking sheet with the melted coconut oil.

3. In a large bowl, combine the chicken strips and coconut milk.

4. In a shallow bowl, mix together the rice flour, salt, onion powder, paprika, mustard powder, and garlic powder.

5. Working one at a time, roll the chicken strips in the flour mixture and then place them on the baking sheet.

6. Place the sheet in the preheated oven and bake for 15 minutes.

7. Serve with Honey-Mustard-Sesame Sauce for dipping.

- PALEO
- MEDITERRANEAN

COOKING TIP: To make these chicken fingers extra crispy, brush the tops of the coated chicken strips with melted coconut oil before baking.

ACTION PLAN TIP: If you're using this recipe as part of the Paleo Action Plan, double the quantities so you have enough leftovers for later in the week.

PER SERVING
Calories: 762; Total Fat: 35g; Total Carbohydrates: 67g; Sugar: 26g; Fiber: 3g; Protein: 47g; Sodium: 1074mg

Easy Turkey Breakfast Sausage

SERVES 4 / PREP TIME: 15 MINUTES / COOK TIME: 15 MINUTES

• PALEO

• MEDITERRANEAN

RECIPE TIP: One serving equals 3 sausage patties, leaving plenty to refrigerate or freeze for future breakfasts and snacks.

ACTION PLAN TIP: If you're using this recipe as part of the Paleo Action Plan, double the quantities so you have enough leftovers for later in the week.

PER SERVING

Calories: 348; Total Fat: 19g; Total Carbohydrates: 4g; Sugar: 2g; Fiber: 1g; Protein: 47g; Sodium: 765mg

Although called "breakfast" sausage, this really can be "anytime" sausage. And if you avoid eggs, sausage is a good protein alternative. Most commercially available breakfast sausages are loaded with ingredients that don't support anti-inflammatory eating. Making your own is easy. These are fast and can be stored in the refrigerator to reheat whenever you want. If you can't find dried blueberries, dried cranberries or cherries can be substituted. This recipe makes about 24 sausage patties.

Extra-virgin olive oil, for brushing

1½ pounds ground turkey

1 teaspoon salt

½ teaspoon freshly ground black pepper

½ teaspoon ground nutmeg

1 tablespoon chopped fresh sage

2 scallions, sliced

½ cup dried blueberries

1. Preheat the oven to 400°F.

2. Brush a rimmed baking sheet with olive oil.

3. In a medium bowl, mix together the turkey, salt, pepper, nutmeg, sage, scallions, and blueberries; it may be easiest to do this with your hands.

4. Using a small (1-ounce) ice cream scoop, scoop the mixture onto the prepared baking sheet. With your fingers or the back of a spatula, gently flatten the mounds into a patty shape.

5. Place the sheet in the preheated oven and bake for 10 to 15 minutes, or until firm to the touch.

Garlic-Mustard Lamb Chops

SERVES 4 / PREP TIME: 30 MINUTES / COOK TIME: 20 MINUTES

In this classic French preparation, lamb chops are rubbed with a garlic-mustard sauce. These are wonderful served on a bed of Cauliflower Purée (page 163), or with wild rice and sautéed chard.

8 (4- to 5-ounce) lamb loin chops

2 tablespoons chopped fresh oregano

4 garlic cloves, mashed

¼ cup extra-virgin olive oil

1 teaspoon Dijon mustard

1 teaspoon salt

¼ teaspoon freshly ground black pepper

1. Place the lamb chops in a shallow baking dish.

2. In a small bowl, whisk together the oregano, garlic, olive oil, Dijon mustard, salt, and pepper.

3. Rub the mixture over the lamb chops. Cover the dish with plastic wrap and marinate the chops at room temperature for 30 minutes.

4. Preheat the oven to 425°F.

5. Remove the plastic wrap and place the dish in the preheated oven. Bake the lamb chops for 15 to 20 minutes, or until they are sizzling and browned.

6. Let the chops sit for 5 minutes before serving.

• PALEO

• MEDITERRANEAN

COOKING TIP: Letting the chops sit for 5 minutes before serving will keep them juicy.

TIME-SAVING TIP: Refrigerate and marinate the lamb chops in the mustard sauce overnight. Bring them to room temperature before putting them in the preheated oven.

PER SERVING

Calories: 648; Total Fat: 34g; Total Carbohydrates: 3g; Sugar: 0g; Fiber: 1g; Protein: 80g; Sodium: 812mg

Spicy Chicken Drumsticks

SERVES 4 TO 6 / PREP TIME: 10 MINUTES / COOK TIME: 35 TO 45 MINUTES

• PALEO

• MEDITERRANEAN

COOKING TIP: It's hard to overcook chicken drumsticks because the bone keeps them moist. If you're not sure whether the meat is cooked, keep them in the oven for an additional 10 minutes. If the skin is already brown, cover the pan with foil for the extra time.

PER SERVING

Calories: 380; Total Fat: 31g; Total Carbohydrates: 9g; Sugar: 5g; Fiber: 2g; Protein: 19g; Sodium: 686mg

Nondairy yogurt and anti-inflammatory spices coat these drumsticks. They are best when marinated overnight; if you don't have the time, give them at least 30 minutes before cooking. Try this marinade on chicken wings, too.

6 chicken drumsticks

1 cup unsweetened coconut yogurt

½ cup extra-virgin olive oil

Juice of 2 limes

2 garlic cloves, smashed

1 tablespoon raw honey

1 teaspoon salt

1 teaspoon ground cumin

½ teaspoon paprika

½ teaspoon ground turmeric

¼ teaspoon freshly ground black pepper

Olive oil cooking spray

1. Place the chicken in a shallow baking dish.

2. In a small bowl, whisk together the yogurt, olive oil, lime juice, garlic, honey, salt, cumin, paprika, turmeric, and pepper until smooth.

3. Pour the yogurt mixture over the chicken. Cover with plastic wrap and chill for 30 minutes, or overnight.

4. Preheat the oven to 375°F.

5. Line a rimmed baking sheet with aluminum foil and lightly grease it with cooking spray.

6. Remove the drumsticks from the marinade and place them on the prepared sheet. Discard the marinade.

7. Place the sheet in the preheated oven and bake the drumsticks for 25 to 35 minutes, or until they start to brown and are cooked through.

Lamb Stew

SERVES 4 TO 6 / PREP TIME: 15 MINUTES / COOK TIME: 8 HOURS

• PALEO

• MEDITERRANEAN

• TIME-SAVING

STORAGE TIP: Lamb stew makes great leftovers since the flavors improve the next day. It's also perfect for doubling the batch and freezing for future meals.

ACTION PLAN TIP: If you're using this recipe as part of the Paleo, Mediterranean, or Time-Saving Action Plan double the quantities so you have enough leftovers for later in the week.

PER SERVING

Calories: 595; Total Fat: 24g; Total Carbohydrates: 19g; Sugar: 6g; Fiber: 8g; Protein: 72g; Sodium: 1591mg

This is classic, homey, comforting lamb stew. For a creamy version, replace 1 cup of chicken broth with 1 cup of coconut milk. This stew is delicious ladled over gluten-free pasta or served with Cauliflower Purée (page 163).

1 tablespoon extra-virgin olive oil
½ cup coconut flour
1 tablespoon paprika
1 teaspoon salt
½ teaspoon freshly ground black pepper
2 pounds lamb stew meat

1 onion, sliced
3 garlic cloves, smashed
4 carrots, cut into 2-inch pieces
4 cups chicken broth
1 bay leaf
2 fresh rosemary sprigs

1. To the slow cooker, add the olive oil.

2. In a large bowl, mix together the coconut flour, paprika, salt, and pepper. Add the lamb and toss to coat. Transfer the lamb to the slow cooker.

3. Cover the lamb with the onion, garlic, carrots, chicken broth, bay leaf, and rosemary. Cover the cooker and cook on low for 8 hours.

4. Remove and discard the bay leaf and rosemary sprigs before serving.

Lentil-Lamb Ragu

SERVES 4 / PREP TIME: 10 MINUTES / COOK TIME: 30 MINUTES

While delicious right out of the pot, the flavors only get better the next day—making this the perfect make-ahead recipe. Enjoy over zucchini noodles or with roasted spaghetti squash.

2 tablespoons extra-virgin olive oil

1 red onion, chopped

4 garlic cloves, minced

1 pound lean ground lamb

1 (14-ounce) can chopped tomatoes

1 cup chicken broth, plus additional as needed

½ cup green lentils

1 teaspoon salt

1 teaspoon dried oregano

1 teaspoon ground cumin

½ teaspoon freshly ground black pepper

• MEDITERRANEAN
• TIME-SAVING

Sensitivity Alert

PALEO TIP: Omit the lentils and replace with 1 cup of finely chopped mushrooms.

ACTION PLAN TIP: If you're using this recipe as part of the Mediterranean Action Plan, double the quantities so you have enough leftovers for later in the week.

PER SERVING

Calories: 402; Total Fat: 16g; Total Carbohydrates: 23g; Sugar: 5g; Fiber: 10g; Protein: 41g; Sodium: 867mg

1. In a large pan over high heat, heat the olive oil. Add the onion and sauté for 3 minutes. Add the garlic and sauté for 1 minute.

2. Add the ground lamb, breaking it up with a spoon. Cook for 3 to 4 minutes, or until the lamb is browned.

3. Stir in the tomatoes, chicken broth, lentils, salt, oregano, cumin, and pepper. Simmer for 20 minutes, or until the lentils are cooked and most the liquid has evaporated. If the lentils are not yet tender and most of the liquid has evaporated, stir in a little more broth or some water.

12

Desserts

Melon *with* Berry-Yogurt Sauce

SERVES 6 / PREP TIME: 15 MINUTES

- VEGAN
- PALEO
- MEDITERRANEAN
- TIME-SAVING

RECIPE TIP: The mashed berries are great on pancakes and waffles.

PER SERVING

Calories: 76; Total Fat: 4g; Total Carbohydrates: 11g; Sugar: 5g; Fiber: 6g; Protein: 1g; Sodium: 37mg

This simple sauce turns plain melon into a special treat; the toasted coconut provides a nice texture. This is great for breakfast or brunch, as well as dessert. If cantaloupe isn't in season, substitute any ripe melon.

1 cantaloupe, peeled and sliced

1 pint fresh raspberries

½ teaspoon vanilla extract

1 cup plain coconut or almond yogurt

½ cup toasted coconut

1. Arrange the melon slices on a serving plate.

2. In a small bowl, mash the berries with the vanilla. Add the yogurt and stir until just mixed.

3. Spoon the berry-yogurt mixture over the melon slices and sprinkle with the coconut.

Roasted Peaches *with* Raspberry Sauce *and* Coconut Cream

SERVES 4 / PEP TIME: 15 MINUTES / COOK TIME: 15 MINUTES

A classic Peach Melba—peaches with raspberry sauce—is a delicious way to enjoy fresh peaches. Roasting peaches intensifies their flavor, the raspberry sauce adds tartness, and the coconut cream and pistachios make this simple dessert divine.

4 peaches, almost ripe, halved

2 tablespoons coconut oil, melted

1 (10-ounce) bag frozen no-added-sugar raspberries, thawed

½ cup Coconut Cream (page 266)

2 tablespoons chopped pistachios

1. Preheat the oven to 400°F.

2. In a shallow baking dish, place the peaches and brush them with the melted coconut oil.

3. Place the dish in the preheated oven and roast the peaches for 10 to 15 minutes, or until they begin to brown.

4. While the peaches are roasting, purée the raspberries in a food processor. If you don't like seeds in your raspberry sauce, strain it through a fine-mesh strainer.

5. To serve, place the peaches on a serving platter, cut-side up. Top with Coconut Cream, drizzle with raspberry sauce, and sprinkle with the pistachios.

- VEGAN
- PALEO
- MEDITERRANEAN

Sensitivity Alert

MEDITERRANEAN TIP:
If you're following the Mediterranean Action Plan, substitute softened goat cheese for the Coconut Cream.

PER SERVING
Calories: 261; Total Fat: 16g; Total Carbohydrates: 31g; Sugar: 25g; Fiber: 6g; Protein: 3g; Sodium: 5mg

Cherry Ice Cream

SERVES 4 TO 6 / PREP TIME: 10 MINUTES

- VEGAN
- PALEO
- MEDITERRANEAN
- TIME-SAVING

Sensitivity Alert

VARIATION TIP: For a creamier texture replace the almond milk with coconut milk. If you'd like it sweeter, add ¼ cup of raw honey or maple syrup.

PER SERVING

Calories: 82; Total Fat: 2g; Total Carbohydrates: 14g; Sugar: 12g; Fiber: 2g; Protein: 1g; Sodium: 121mg

Refreshing, fruity, and icy cold, this is a fast and easy frozen dessert. For an even tastier treat, serve it with toasted almonds and chunks of bittersweet chocolate. It is best eaten within a few days of making as it tends to get icy if kept longer. This recipe can be made with any frozen fruit you like.

1 (10-ounce) package frozen no-added-sugar cherries

3 cups unsweetened almond milk

1 teaspoon vanilla extract

½ teaspoon almond extract

1. In a blender or food processor, combine the cherries, almond milk, vanilla extract, and almond extract. Process until mostly smooth; a few chunks of cherries are fine.

2. Pour the mixture into a container with an airtight lid. Freeze thoroughly before serving.

Blueberry Crisp

SERVES 4 / PREP TIME: 15 MINUTES / COOK TIME: 20 MINUTES

This crisp can be made with fresh or frozen berries and you can substitute whatever berry or fruit you prefer. With almost no sugar, you can feel virtuous eating it. Leftovers make a great breakfast. Eat dessert first!

½ cup coconut oil, melted, plus additional for brushing
1 quart fresh blueberries
¼ cup maple syrup
Juice of ½ lemon

2 teaspoons lemon zest
1 cup gluten-free rolled oats
½ teaspoon ground cinnamon
½ cup chopped pecans
Pinch salt

1. Preheat the oven to 350°F.

2. Brush a shallow baking dish with melted coconut oil. Stir together the blueberries, maple syrup, lemon juice, and lemon zest in the dish.

3. In a small bowl, combine the oats, ½ cup of melted coconut oil, cinnamon, pecans, and salt. Mix the ingredients well to evenly distribute the coconut oil. Sprinkle the oat mixture over the berries.

4. Place the dish in the preheated oven and bake for 20 minutes, or until the oats are lightly browned.

• VEGAN
• MEDITERRANEAN

Sensitivity Alert

SUBSTITUTION TIP: Rolled oats can be replaced with quinoa flakes.

PER SERVING
Calories: 497; Total Fat: 33g; Total Carbohydrates: 51g; Sugar: 26g; Fiber: 7g; Protein: 5g; Sodium: 42mg

Grilled Pineapple
with Chocolate Ganache

SERVES 6 / PREP TIME: 30 MINUTES / COOK TIME: 15 MINUTES

Grilling pineapple wedges brings out their juices and adds a smoky flavor—and everyone loves dipping things into chocolate. Chocolate ganache has many uses: as a filling for cookies, frosting for cake, and a sauce for ice cream. It's easy to make and can be kept in the freezer for months.

- VEGAN
- PALEO
- MEDITERRANEAN

PER SERVING
Calories: 462; Total Fat: 23g;
Total Carbohydrates: 61g;
Sugar: 48g; Fiber: 2g;
Protein: 5g; Sodium: 5mg

FOR THE GANACHE
½ cup coconut milk
1½ cups semi-sweet or bittersweet chocolate morsels

FOR THE PINEAPPLE
1 pineapple, peeled, cored, and cut into 16 wedges
1 tablespoon coconut oil, melted
1 tablespoon coconut sugar
1 teaspoon chopped fresh rosemary

To make the ganache

1. In a medium saucepan over medium-high heat, add the coconut milk. Heat the milk until it just begins to scald (little bubbles or foam will begin to collect around the perimeter of the pan).

2. Remove the pan from the heat and add the chocolate. Let stand for 1 minute.

3. Whisk the mixture until it's smooth and satiny. ⇒

Grilled Pineapple with Chocolate Ganache

CONTINUED

....

To make the pineapple

1. Preheat an indoor stove-top grill until very hot.

2. Brush the pineapple wedges with melted coconut oil.

3. Grill the wedges for 1 to 2 minutes per side, or until grill marks appear.

4. Arrange the pineapple on a serving platter and sprinkle with the coconut sugar and rosemary.

5. Serve with the ganache.

Chocolate-Avocado Mousse *with* Sea Salt

SERVES 4 TO 6 / PREP TIME: 10 MINUTES / COOK TIME: 5 MINUTES

. . . .

Rich and smooth, the texture of this mousse is silky and decadent. The bittersweet chocolate and the avocado combine beautifully and the dusting of sea salt intensifies the flavors. It's a healthy dessert or snack as the avocados provide healthy fats and proteins and cocoa is good for blood pressure. Seconds, anyone?

8 ounces bittersweet chocolate, chopped

¼ cup coconut milk

2 tablespoons coconut oil

2 ripe avocados

¼ cup raw honey or maple syrup

Pinch sea salt

1. In a small heavy saucepan over low heat, combine the chocolate, coconut milk, and coconut oil. Cook for 2 to 3 minutes, stirring constantly, or until the chocolate melts.

2. In a food processor, combine the avocado and honey. Add the melted chocolate and process until smooth.

3. Spoon the mousse into serving bowls and top each with a sprinkle of sea salt. Chill for at least 30 minutes before serving.

- VEGAN
- PALEO
- MEDITERRANEAN
- TIME-SAVING

STORAGE TIP: It's best to eat this mousse within three days of making it; any longer and the liquid in the avocado will begin to separate from the solids.

VEGAN TIP: If you're following the Vegan Action Plan, use the coconut sugar or maple syrup in place of the honey.

PER SERVING

Calories: 653; Total Fat: 47g; Total Carbohydrates: 56g; Sugar: 42g; Fiber: 9g; Protein: 7g; Sodium: 113mg

Fruit *and* Walnut Crumble

SERVES 6 / PREP TIME: 15 MINUTES / COOK TIME: 15 TO 20 MINUTES

Use seasonal fruits for this dessert; mix and match flavors to see what you like best. Here, blueberries, figs, and nectarines combine for a mouthwatering treat. The topping is a grain-free mixture of nuts and spices. Leftovers are great for breakfast.

- VEGAN
- PALEO
- MEDITERRANEAN

Sensitivity Alert

VEGAN TIP: If you're following the Vegan Action Plan, use the maple syrup instead of the honey.

PER SERVING

Calories: 335; Total Fat: 19g; Total Carbohydrates: 42g; Sugar: 32g; Fiber: 6g; Protein: 6g; Sodium: 32mg

FOR THE TOPPING

1 cup coarsely chopped walnuts

¼ cup coarsely chopped hazelnuts

1 tablespoon ghee or melted coconut oil

1 teaspoon ground cinnamon

Pinch salt

FOR THE FILLING

1 cup fresh blueberries

6 fresh figs, quartered

2 nectarines, pitted and sliced

½ cup coconut sugar, raw honey, or maple syrup

2 teaspoons lemon zest

1 teaspoon vanilla extract

To make the topping

In a small bowl, mix together the walnuts, hazelnuts, ghee, cinnamon, and salt. Set aside.

To make the filling

1. Preheat the oven to 375°F.

2. In a medium bowl, combine the blueberries, figs, nectarines, coconut sugar, lemon zest, and vanilla.

3. Divide the fruit among six ovenproof single-serving bowls or ramekins.

4. Spoon equal amounts of the nut topping over each serving.

5. Place the bowls in the preheated oven and bake for 15 to 20 minutes, or until the nuts brown and the fruit is bubbly.

Coconut Ice Cream Sandwiches

SERVES 6 / PREP TIME: 45 MINUTES / COOK TIME: 15 MINUTES

· ·

- VEGAN
- PALEO
- MEDITERRANEAN

PER SERVING
Calories: 673; Total Fat: 53g;
Total Carbohydrates: 48g;
Sugar: 42g; Fiber: 2g;
Protein: 5g; Sodium: 538mg

Big kids and little kids all love ice cream sandwiches, and these are (almost) guilt free. The cookies do have a touch of coconut sugar in them because it makes them crisp. Coconut sugar is a natural sugar, low on the glycemic charts, which means it takes longer to process in your body than traditional sugars. If you don't have an ice cream maker, use store-bought ice cream; look for a brand that is dairy free, low glycemic, and contains only ingredients you can pronounce.

FOR THE COCONUT
ICE CREAM
4 cups full-fat coconut milk
¾ cup coconut sugar
2 teaspoons vanilla extract

FOR THE COOKIES
2 cups almond flour
3 tablespoons coconut sugar
1 teaspoon salt
½ teaspoon baking soda
¼ teaspoon ground cardamom
6 tablespoons coconut oil,
 melted and cooled slightly
¼ cup maple syrup
1 tablespoon almond milk
1 teaspoon vanilla extract

FOR THE FINISHED
ICE CREAM SANDWICHES
½ cup shredded coconut

To make the coconut ice cream

1. In a large saucepan over medium heat, combine the coconut milk and coconut sugar. Cook for about 5 minutes, stirring constantly, or until the sugar dissolves. Remove the pan from the heat and stir in the vanilla.

2. Chill the mixture for at least 4 hours, or overnight.

3. Make the ice cream according to the manufacturer's instructions for your ice cream maker.

4. Freeze the ice cream in an airtight container.

To make the cookies

1. Preheat the oven to 325°F.

2. Line two baking sheets with parchment paper.

3. In a medium bowl, combine the almond flour, coconut sugar, salt, baking soda, and cardamom.

4. Add the coconut oil, maple syrup, almond milk, and vanilla. Mix until a thick dough forms.

5. Using a spoon, place scoops of dough on the prepared sheets, leaving about 2 inches between each cookie. There should be enough dough for 12 cookies.

6. Gently flatten the cookies with your hand or the back of the spoon.

7. Place the sheets in the preheated oven and bake for 10 to 12 minutes, or until golden brown. Cool the cookies thoroughly before making the ice cream sandwiches.

To assemble the ice cream sandwiches

1. Place a generous scoop of coconut ice cream on the bottom of one cookie and top it with a second cookie, pressing together gently. Individually wrap the cookies and freeze until ready to eat.

2. When ready to serve, press shredded coconut into the ice cream along the edges of each sandwich.

Chocolate-Cherry Clusters

MAKES ABOUT 10 CLUSTERS / PREP TIME: 15 MINUTES

• VEGAN
• PALEO
• MEDITERRANEAN
• TIME-SAVING

Sensitivity Alert

COOKING TIP: If you don't have a double boiler, melt the chocolate and coconut oil in the microwave on 80 percent power, 1 minute at a time, until the chocolate melts.

PER SERVING

Calories: 198; Total Fat: 13g; Total Carbohydrates: 18g; Sugar: 12g; Fiber: 4g; Protein: 4g; Sodium: 58mg

How lovely that both chocolate and cherries are good for us! This healthy alternative to a candy bar will satisfy that sweet tooth when it hits. Store in the refrigerator, but their flavor improves if you let them sit for 30 minutes at room temperature before eating.

1 cup dark chocolate (60 percent cocoa or higher), chopped
1 tablespoon coconut oil
1 cup roasted salted almonds
½ cup dried cherries

1. Line a rimmed baking sheet with wax paper.
2. Over a double boiler, stir together the chocolate and coconut oil until melted and smooth.
3. Remove the pan from the heat and stir in the almonds and cherries.
4. By spoonfuls, drop clusters onto the wax paper. Refrigerate until hardened.
5. Transfer to an airtight container and refrigerate.

Gluten-Free Oat *and* Fruit Bars

MAKES 16 BARS / PREP TIME: 15 MINUTES / COOK TIME: 40 TO 45 MINUTES

A cross between a cookie and a granola bar, these are easy to make and great to have on hand for an on-the-go meal or snack. Add whatever dried fruit you like: blueberries, cranberries, cherries, apricots, raisins, or a combination.

Cooking spray
½ cup maple syrup
½ cup almond or
  sunflower butter
2 medium ripe bananas,
  mashed
⅓ cup dried cranberries
1½ cups old-fashioned
  rolled oats

½ cup shredded coconut
¼ cup oat flour
¼ cup ground flaxseed
1 teaspoon vanilla extract
½ teaspoon ground cinnamon
¼ teaspoon ground cloves

• VEGAN
• MEDITERRANEAN

Sensitivity Alert

STORAGE TIP:
Once cooled, cut into
16 bars. Wrap each
bar in wax paper or
parchment paper and
store in an airtight
container in the
freezer. Wrapping the
bars individually makes
them easier to grab
and go.

PER SERVING
Calories: 144; Total Fat: 7g;
Total Carbohydrates: 19g;
Sugar: 8g; Fiber: 2g;
Protein: 3g; Sodium: 3mg

1. Preheat the oven to 400°F.

2. Line an 8-by-8-inch square pan with parchment paper or aluminum foil, and coat the lined pan with cooking spray.

3. In a medium bowl, combine the maple syrup, almond butter, and bananas. Mix until well blended.

4. Add the cranberries, oats, coconut, oat flour, flaxseed, vanilla, cinnamon, and cloves. Mix well.

5. Spoon the mixture into the prepared pan; the mixture will be thick and sticky. Use an oiled spatula to spread the mixture evenly.

6. Place the pan in the preheated oven and bake for 40 to 45 minutes, or until the top is dry and a toothpick inserted in the middle comes out clean. Cool completely before cutting into bars.

13

Sauces, Condiments, & Dressings

Creamy Coconut-Herb Dressing

MAKES ABOUT 1 CUP / PREP TIME: 5 MINUTES

• VEGAN

• PALEO

• MEDITERRANEAN

• TIME-SAVING

PER SERVING (2 tablespoons)
Calories: 14; Total Fat: 1g;
Total Carbohydrates: 2g;
Sugar: 0g; Fiber: 1g;
Protein: 0g; Sodium: 172mg

Reminiscent of Green Goddess dressing, the lemon juice provides the tang rather than buttermilk. Since the flavors are delicate, it's best to use this dressing within five days of making it.

8 ounces plain coconut yogurt

2 tablespoons freshly squeezed lemon juice

2 tablespoons chopped fresh parsley

1 tablespoon snipped fresh chives

½ teaspoon salt

Pinch freshly ground black pepper

1. In a medium bowl, whisk together the yogurt, lemon juice, parsley, chives, salt, and pepper.

2. Refrigerate in an airtight container.

Avocado Dressing

MAKES ABOUT 2 CUPS / PREP TIME: 10 MINUTES

This dressing is thick and satisfying, and adds healthy fats and protein to your salad. Because it contains avocado it will oxidize and turn brown over time; it's best eaten within several days of making it.

- VEGAN
- PALEO
- MEDITERRANEAN
- TIME-SAVING

1 ripe avocado

1 cup plain coconut yogurt

¼ cup freshly squeezed
  lemon juice

1 scallion, chopped

1 tablespoon chopped
  fresh cilantro

PER SERVING (2 tablespoons)
Calories: 33; Total Fat: 3g;
Total Carbohydrates: 2g;
Sugar: 0g; Fiber: 1g;
Protein: 0g; Sodium: 14mg

1. In a food processor, blend the avocado, yogurt, lemon juice, scallion, and cilantro until smooth.

2. Refrigerate in an airtight container.

Berry Vinaigrette

MAKES ABOUT 1½ CUPS / PREP TIME: 15 MINUTES

- VEGAN
- PALEO
- MEDITERRANEAN
- TIME-SAVING

VEGAN TIP: If you're following the Vegan Action Plan, use the maple syrup instead of the honey.

PER SERVING (2 tablespoons)
Calories: 73; Total Fat: 7g; Total Carbohydrates: 3g; Sugar: 2g; Fiber: 0g; Protein: 0g; Sodium: 210mg

Why not double up your nutrition? This dressing will top your salad with additional anti-inflammatory goodness. Any soft seasonal fruit can replace the berries in this recipe. Give figs or plums a try. For an extra-fruity flavor, use almond or walnut oil in place of the extra-virgin olive oil.

1 cup berries, fresh or frozen, no added sugar (thawed if frozen)

½ cup balsamic vinegar

⅓ cup extra-virgin olive oil

2 tablespoons freshly squeezed lemon or lime juice

1 tablespoon raw honey or maple syrup

1 tablespoon lemon or lime zest

1 tablespoon Dijon mustard

1 teaspoon salt

½ teaspoon freshly ground black pepper

1. In a blender, purée the berries, balsamic vinegar, olive oil, lemon juice, honey, lemon zest, Dijon mustard, salt, and pepper until smooth.

2. Refrigerate in an airtight container for up to five days.

Almost Caesar Salad Dressing

MAKES ABOUT 1 CUP / PREP TIME: 10 MINUTES

• PALEO

• MEDITERRANEAN

• TIME-SAVING

VEGAN TIP: If you're following the Vegan Action Plan, omit the anchovy fillets and replace them with 2 tablespoons chopped pitted olives.

PER SERVING (2 tablespoons)
Calories: 166; Total Fat: 19g; Total Carbohydrates: 0g; Sugar: 0g; Fiber: 0g; Protein: 0g; Sodium: 184mg

Hail Caesar! This recipe has all of the flavor of traditional Caesar dressing but none of the dairy or eggs—it's also great as a vegetable dip. If you can find salt-cured anchovies, they make the best Caesar dressing. If using, rinse off the excess salt before adding them to the food processor.

¾ cup extra-virgin olive oil

3 tablespoons apple cider vinegar

2 anchovy fillets

2 garlic cloves, minced

½ teaspoon salt

Freshly ground black pepper

1. In a blender or food processor, purée the olive oil, cider vinegar, anchovies, garlic, salt, and pepper until smooth.

2. Refrigerate in an airtight container and use within one week.

Cherry-Peach Chutney *with* Mint

MAKES ABOUT 2 CUPS / PREP TIME: 15 MINUTES

This summer-tasting chutney is delicious with roasted winter squash, wild rice, and grilled or roasted chicken. It's great with fresh peaches, but you will need to peel and chop them. The dried cherries plump as they soak up the peach juices in the chutney.

- VEGAN
- PALEO
- MEDITERRANEAN
- TIME-SAVING

COOKING TIP: The mint is added at the very last minute so it isn't oxidized by the acids in the chutney.

VEGAN TIP: If you're following the Vegan Action Plan, use the maple syrup instead of the honey.

1 (10-ounce) bag frozen no-added-sugar peach chunks, thawed, drained, coarsely chopped, juice reserved

½ medium red onion, diced

¼ cup dried cherries, coarsely chopped

2 tablespoons freshly squeezed lemon juice

1 tablespoon raw honey or maple syrup

1 teaspoon apple cider vinegar

¼ teaspoon salt

1 tablespoon chopped fresh mint leaves

1. Place the peach chunks in a medium bowl.

2. Stir in the onion, cherries, lemon juice, honey, cider vinegar, and salt.

3. Let the mixture stand for 30 minutes before serving.

4. When ready to serve, stir in the mint.

5. Refrigerate in an airtight container for no more than three days.

PER SERVING (¼ cup)
Calories: 42; Total Fat: 0g; Total Carbohydrates: 10g; Sugar: 7g; Fiber: 2g; Protein: 1g; Sodium: 76mg

Rosemary-Apricot Marinade

MAKES ABOUT 2 CUPS / PREP TIME: 15 MINUTES

Rosemary and apricots are classic Mediterranean flavors and pair beautifully with lamb. In addition to lamb, use this fragrant marinade for chicken or salmon, or as a dressing over roasted butternut squash.

- VEGAN
- PALEO
- MEDITERRANEAN
- TIME-SAVING

1 cup chopped apricots, fresh or frozen

½ red onion, quartered

½ cup extra-virgin olive oil

¼ cup apple cider vinegar

2 garlic cloves

2 tablespoons raw honey or maple syrup

1 tablespoon Dijon mustard

2 teaspoons chopped fresh rosemary

1 teaspoon salt

¼ teaspoon freshly ground black pepper

1. In a blender or food processor, combine the apricots, onion, olive oil, cider vinegar, garlic, honey, Dijon mustard, rosemary, salt, and pepper. Process until smooth. (It's fine to see flecks of rosemary and red onion.)

2. Refrigerate in an airtight container for up to five days.

COOKING TIP: When using as a marinade, allow the foods to soak in the dressing for at least 30 minutes before cooking; for the best flavor marinate overnight.

VEGAN TIP: If you're following the Vegan Action Plan, use the maple syrup instead of the honey.

PER SERVING (2 tablespoons) Calories: 69; Total Fat: 6g; Total Carbohydrates: 3g; Sugar: 3g; Fiber: 0g; Protein: 0g; Sodium: 159mg

Green Olive Tapenade

MAKES ABOUT 1 CUP / PREP TIME: 10 MINUTES

· ·

- VEGAN
- PALEO
- MEDITERRANEAN
- TIME-SAVING

PER SERVING (2 tablespoons)
Calories: 73; Total Fat: 8g;
Total Carbohydrates: 2g;
Sugar: 0g; Fiber: 1g;
Protein: 0g; Sodium: 201mg

Tapenade is an excellent condiment to have on hand. It has a good shelf life and a few tablespoons add flavor and interest to grilled meats and vegetables, or add garlicky saltiness to sauces and salad dressings.

1 cup pitted green olives

2 garlic cloves

¼ cup extra-virgin olive oil

¼ cup freshly squeezed lemon juice

Pinch dried rosemary

Salt

Freshly ground black pepper

1. In a food processor, combine the olives, garlic, olive oil, lemon juice, and rosemary. Season with salt and pepper. Process until the mixture is almost smooth; a little chunky is fine.

2. Refrigerate in an airtight container. The tapenade will keep for several weeks.

Kale Pesto

MAKES ABOUT 1 CUP / PREP TIME: 15 MINUTES

Kale replaces basil in this classic recipe. This pesto is delicious served with roasted winter squash or as a dip for Sweet Potato Chips (page 124). Try stirring some into your favorite gluten-free pasta.

- VEGAN
- PALEO
- MEDITERRANEAN
- TIME-SAVING

Sensitivity Alert

2 cups chopped kale leaves, thoroughly washed and stemmed

½ cup toasted almonds

2 garlic cloves

3 tablespoons freshly squeezed lemon juice

3 tablespoons extra-virgin olive oil

2 teaspoons lemon zest

1 teaspoon salt

½ teaspoon freshly ground black pepper

¼ teaspoon red pepper flakes

SUBSTITUTION TIP: If you don't like kale, swap in an equal amount of spinach. The almonds can be replaced with any other nut you like.

1. In a food processor, combine the kale, almonds, garlic, lemon juice, olive oil, lemon zest, salt, black pepper, and red pepper flakes. Process until smooth.

2. Refrigerate in an airtight container for up to one week.

PER SERVING (2 tablespoons) Calories: 91; Total Fat: 8g; Total Carbohydrates: 4g; Sugar: 0g; Fiber: 1g; Protein: 2g; Sodium: 299mg

Honey-Mustard-Sesame Sauce

MAKES ABOUT 1 CUP / PREP TIME: 10 MINUTES

- VEGAN
- PALEO
- MEDITERRANEAN
- TIME-SAVING

INGREDIENT TIP: If the raw honey is solid, warm it slightly before combining it with the other ingredients.

VEGAN TIP: If you're following the Vegan Action Plan, use the maple syrup instead of the honey.

PER SERVING (2 tablespoons)
Calories: 67; Total Fat: 1g;
Total Carbohydrates: 14g;
Sugar: 12g; Fiber: 1g;
Protein: 1g; Sodium: 179mg

A simple but delicious blend of mustard, honey, and sesame, this sauce is good on salads, vegetables, and meats—and a perfect dipper for Chicken Fingers (page 227). It will last several weeks in the refrigerator.

½ cup Dijon mustard

½ cup raw honey or maple syrup

1 garlic clove, minced

1 teaspoon toasted sesame oil

1. In a small bowl, whisk together the Dijon, honey, garlic, and sesame oil.
2. Refrigerate in an airtight container.

Chia Jam

MAKES ABOUT 3 CUPS / PREP TIME: 15 MINUTES

The thickening power of chia makes a jam-like texture in this healthy alternative to sugary preserves. Use any berries or fruit, fresh or frozen, to make this jam. Chia jam is good on pancakes, waffles, grilled fruit, or served with yogurt.

1 pound ripe fresh berries
1 teaspoon vanilla extract

3 tablespoons chia seeds

1. In a food processor, purée the berries and vanilla until smooth.

2. Add the chia seeds and pulse for 10 seconds.

3. Place the jam in a pint jar (or two), seal tightly, and refrigerate. Consume within one week.

• VEGAN
• PALEO
• MEDITERRANEAN
• TIME-SAVING

PER SERVING (2 tablespoons)
Calories: 10; Total Fat: 0g;
Total Carbohydrates: 2g;
Sugar: 1g; Fiber: 1g;
Protein: 0g; Sodium: 0mg

Slow-Cooker Ghee

MAKES ABOUT 2 CUPS / PREP TIME: 5 MINUTES / COOK TIME: 2 HOURS

- PALEO
- MEDITERRANEAN
- TIME-SAVING

INGREDIENT TIP: You can make ghee with either salted or unsalted butter. If using salted butter, note that most of the salt ends up in the solids and is discarded; however, there will still be a light saltiness to the ghee. When making ghee, use the best-quality butter you can source, ideally organic, from pastured, grass-fed cows.

COOKING TIP: The length of time needed for the butter to brown will vary from slow cooker to slow cooker. The first time you make it, stay close in case it cooks faster than noted in this recipe. It can also take much longer.

PER SERVING (1 tablespoon)
Calories: 102; Total Fat: 12g;
Total Carbohydrates: 0g;
Sugar: 0g; Fiber: 0g;
Protein: 0g; Sodium: 82mg

Ghee is butter that has undergone a long, slow cooking process, which results in the solids separating from the oil. For people with dairy sensitivity, it is typically the solids in dairy products that cause the allergic reaction. Even those who are dairy intolerant can enjoy the buttery flavor of ghee. Ghee also has a higher smoke point than butter, which makes it good for sautéing. In addition, it contributes vitamins A, D, E, and is good for digestion.

1 pound (4 sticks) unsalted butter

1. In the slow cooker, add the butter. Set the slow cooker to high and leave it uncovered.

2. In about 45 minutes a white foam should appear. Over time, from 1 to 2 hours, this foam will turn golden brown and give off a pleasant nutty smell. The amount of time this takes depends on your slow cooker.

3. Once the foam has turned brown, turn off the slow cooker.

4. Line a strainer with a triple thickness of cheesecloth and place the strainer over a wide-mouth jar.

5. Using a large spoon or ladle, skim off as much of the brown foam as possible and discard it. Carefully ladle the remaining ghee into the cheesecloth-lined strainer.

6. Once all the ghee has been strained, discard the cheese-cloth and let the ghee come to room temperature before covering the jar with an airtight lid and refrigerating it. It will keep for three months.

Coconut Cream

MAKES ABOUT 2 CUPS / PREP TIME: 10 MINUTES

- VEGAN
- PALEO
- MEDITERRANEAN

PER SERVING (¼ cup)
Calories: 71; Total Fat: 5g;
Total Carbohydrates: 8g;
Sugar: 7g; Fiber: 0g;
Protein: 0g; Sodium: 4mg

A fun alternative to whipped cream, this only works if everything is very cold and the coconut cream has a very high fat content. It's the cold coconut fat that helps it to whip. Carefully spoon the coconut cream out of the can, trying not to mix it too much as you place it in the chilled bowl.

1 (5.4-ounce) can full-fat coconut cream, refrigerated overnight

¼ cup maple syrup

1 teaspoon vanilla extract

1. Place a medium bowl and the mixer beaters in the refrigerator or freezer for several hours, or until very cold.

2. Into the chilled bowl, spoon the chilled coconut cream. Add the maple syrup and vanilla. Beat with the chilled beaters on high speed until soft peaks form.

3. Refrigerate, covered, until ready to use. It will only hold its peaks for several days.

Slow-Cooker Vegetable Broth

MAKES 6 TO 7 CUPS / PREP TIME: 10 MINUTES / COOK TIME: 6 HOURS

Making your own broth is always more flavorful than using store-bought versions. It's so easy to make and store, it's perfect to have on hand to add a flavor boost when needed. You'll taste the difference right away. And, to make a super anti-inflammatory drink, float a few slices of ginger and turmeric root in a cup of hot broth. Breathe in the aroma, relax, and enjoy.

- VEGAN
- PALEO
- MEDITERRANEAN
- TIME-SAVING

STORAGE TIP: Freeze the broth in 1-cup canning jars for easier use.

VARIATION TIP: To make chicken broth, add 2 pounds of chicken bones to the slow cooker with the other ingredients.

2 leeks, halved lengthwise
1 fennel bulb, halved
1 onion, halved
2 carrots, cut into 2-inch pieces
1 garlic head, halved widthwise

3 fresh parsley sprigs
1 fresh rosemary sprig
1 tablespoon apple cider vinegar
6 cups water

1. In the slow cooker, combine the leeks, fennel, onion, carrots, garlic, parsley, rosemary, cider vinegar, and water. Cook on high for 6 hours.

2. Strain the broth through a fine-mesh strainer and discard any solids.

3. Store the broth in airtight containers in the refrigerator or freezer.

PER SERVING (1 cup)
Calories: 36; Total Fat: 0g; Total Carbohydrates: 5g; Sugar: 1g; Fiber: 1g; Protein: 1g; Sodium: 21mg

Acknowledgments

DOROTHY

By great fortune, I was born into a large Greek family filled with good cooks and people whose green thumbs ensured we always had fresh ingredients readily available. "Cooking from scratch" didn't have meaning, because everything we cooked naturally just came from the fields. My childhood experiences engendered in me a deep respect for food and cooking, which has sustained me both physically and professionally throughout my entire life.

In addition, I'd like to thank and acknowledge my husband, Bob, my daughter, Claire, and all the family and friends who gather regularly around my table. Thanks also go to my editor, Clara Song Lee, for her patience and grace, and the entire Callisto Media team. Lastly, thanks to my junior-high friend, Tom Hanks, whose visits for crêpes and Fleetwood Mac inspired my culinary journey those many years ago.

SONDI

I believe that building health is a group activity, nourished by the wisdom, insight, knowledge, and love of those around us. I'm grateful to all the healers in my life: my husband, family, friends, complementary medicine practitioners, mentors, teachers, chefs, physicians, fellow writers, entrepreneurs, and those I've yet to meet. I'm fortunate to have people around who tell me what they think, not what I want to hear—so thank you for challenging me to grow and change, instead of clinging to comfort.

I want to express special appreciation for my mom, who loves me more than anyone else—even more than my dog (and my dog thinks I'm the most awesome person ever).

Conversion Tables

VOLUME EQUIVALENTS (LIQUID)

US STANDARD	US STANDARD (OUNCES)	METRIC (APPROXIMATE)
2 tablespoons	1 fl. oz.	30 mL
¼ cup	2 fl. oz.	60 mL
½ cup	4 fl. oz.	120 mL
1 cup	8 fl. oz.	240 mL
1½ cups	12 fl. oz.	355 mL
2 cups or 1 pint	16 fl. oz.	475 mL
4 cups or 1 quart	32 fl. oz.	1 L
1 gallon	128 fl. oz.	4 L

OVEN TEMPERATURES

FAHRENHEIT (F)	CELSIUS (C) (APPROXIMATE)
250°	120°
300°	150°
325°	165°
350°	180°
375°	190°
400°	200°
425°	220°
450°	230°

VOLUME EQUIVALENTS (DRY)

US STANDARD	METRIC (APPROXIMATE)
⅛ teaspoon	0.5 mL
¼ teaspoon	1 mL
½ teaspoon	2 mL
¾ teaspoon	4 mL
1 teaspoon	5 mL
1 tablespoon	15 mL
¼ cup	59 mL
⅓ cup	79 mL
½ cup	118 mL
⅔ cup	156 mL
¾ cup	177 mL
1 cup	235 mL
2 cups or 1 pint	475 mL
3 cups	700 mL
4 cups or 1 quart	1 L

WEIGHT EQUIVALENTS

US STANDARD	METRIC (APPROXIMATE)
½ ounce	15 g
1 ounce	30 g
2 ounces	60 g
4 ounces	115 g
8 ounces	225 g
12 ounces	340 g
16 ounces or 1 pound	455 g

The Dirty Dozen & the Clean Fifteen

A nonprofit and environmental watchdog organization called Environmental Working Group (EWG) looks at data supplied by the US Department of Agriculture (USDA) and the Food and Drug Administration (FDA) about pesticide residues. Each year it compiles a list of the best and worst pesticide loads found in commercial crops. You can use these lists to decide which fruits and vegetables to buy organic to minimize your exposure to pesticides and which produce is considered safe enough to buy conventionally. This does not mean they are pesticide-free, though, so wash these fruits and vegetables thoroughly.

These lists change every year, so make sure you look up the most recent one before you fill your shopping cart. You'll find the most recent lists as well as a guide to pesticides in produce at EWG.org/FoodNews.

2015 DIRTY DOZEN

Apples
Celery
Cherry tomatoes
Cucumbers
Grapes
Nectarines (imported)

Peaches
Potatoes
Snap peas (imported)
Spinach
Strawberries
Sweet bell peppers

In addition to the dirty dozen, the EWG added two more produce items contaminated with highly toxic organo-phosphate insecticides:

Kale/Collard greens
Hot peppers

2015 CLEAN FIFTEEN

Asparagus
Avocados
Cabbage
Cantaloupes (domestic)
Cauliflower

Eggplants
Grapefruits
Kiwis
Mangos
Onions

Papayas
Pineapples
Sweet corn
Sweet peas (frozen)
Sweet potatoes

References

BOOKS AND JOURNALS

Barnes, Peter J. "How Corticosteroids Control Inflammation: Quintiles Prize Lecture 2005." *British Journal of Pharmacology* 148, no. 3 (June 2006): 245–254. doi:10.1038/sj.bjp.0706736.

Bateson-Koch, Carolee. *Allergies: Disease in Disguise*. Summertown, TN: Alive Books, 1994.

Chun, O. K., S. J. Chung, K. J. Claycombe, and W. O. Song. "Serum C-Reactive Protein Concentrations Are Inversely Associated with Dietary Flavonoid Intake in U.S. Adults." *Journal of Nutrition* 138, no. 4 (April 2008): 753–60.

Colbin, Annemarie. *Food and Healing*. New York: Random House, 1986.

Erasmus, Udo. *Fats that Heal, Fats that Kill*. Summertown, TN: Alive Books, 1986, 1993.

Esposito, K., F. Nappo, R. Marfella, G. Giugliano, F. Giugliano, M. Ciotola, L. Quagliaro, A., et al. "Inflammatory Cytokine Concentrations Are Acutely Increased by Hyperglycemia in Humans: Role of Oxidative Stress." *Circulation* 106, no. 16 (October 15, 2002): 2067–72.

Estruch, Ramón, Emilio Ros, Jordi Salas-Salvadó, Maria-Isabel Covas, Dolores Corella, Fernando Arós, Enrique Gómez-Gracia, et al. "Primary Prevention of Cardiovascular Disease with a Mediterranean Diet." *New England Journal of Medicine* 368 (April 4, 2013) 1279–90. doi:10.1056/NEJMoa1200303.

Fernandez-Cornejo, Jorge, Seth Wechsler, Mike Livingston, and Lorraine Mitchell. "Genetically Engineered Crops in the United States." ERR-162 (February 2014) 9. US Department of Agriculture, Economic Research Service.

Kaptoge, Stephen, Sreenivasa Rao Kondapally Seshasai, Pei Gao, Daniel F. Freitag, Adam S. Butterworth, Anders Borglykke, Emanuele Di Angelantonio, et al. "Inflammatory Cytokines and Risk of Coronary Heart Disease: New Prospective Study and Updated Meta-Analysis." *European Heart Journal.* 35, no. 9 (March 1, 2014): 578–89. doi:10.1093/eurheartj/eht367.

Libby, Peter. "Inflammation and Cardiovascular Disease Mechanisms." *American Journal of Clinical Nutrition* 83, no. 2 (February 2006): 456S–60S.

Lipski, Elizabeth. *Digestive Wellness*. 3rd ed. New York: McGraw-Hill, 2005.

Mateljan, George. *The World's Healthiest Foods*. Seattle, WA: George Mateljan Foundation, 2007.

Molodecky, N., I. S. Soon, D. M. Rabi, W. A. Ghali, M. Ferris, G. Chernoff, E. I. Benchimol, et al. "Increasing Incidence and Prevalence of the Inflammatory Bowel Diseases with Time, Based on Systematic Review." *Gastroenterology* 142, no. 1 (January 2012): 46–54.e42. doi:10.1053/j.gastro.2011.10.001.

Morris, Alanna, Dorothy Coverson, Lucy Fike, Yusuf Ahmed, Neli Stoyanova, W. Craig Hooper, Gary Gibbons, et al. "Sleep Quality and Duration are Associated with Higher Levels of Inflammatory Biomarkers: the META-Health Study." *Circulation* 122 (2010): A17806.

Mullington, Janet M., Norah S. Simpson, Hans K. Meier-Ewert, and Monika Haack. "Sleep Loss and Inflammation." *Best Practice & Research Clinical Endocrinology & Metabolism* 24, no. 5 (October 2010): 775–84. doi:10.1016/j.beem.2010.08.014.

Murray, Michael and Joseph Pizzorno. *Encyclopedia of Natural Medicine.* 2nd ed. New York: Three Rivers Press, 1998.

Perlmutter, David. *Grain Brain.* New York: Little, Brown and Company, 2013.

Pitchford, Paul. *Healing with Whole Foods.* Berkeley, CA: North Atlantic Books, 2002.

Slavich, George M., and Michael R. Irwin. "From Stress to Inflammation and Major Depressive Disorder: A Social Signal Transduction Theory of Depression." *Psychological Bulletin* 140, no. 3 (May 2014): 774–815. doi:10.1037/a0035302.

Staii, Anca, Sarah Mirocha, Kristina Todorova-Koteva, Simone Glinberg, and Juan C. Jaume. "Hashimoto Thyroiditis Is more Frequent than Expected When Diagnosed by Cytology Which Uncovers a Pre-Clinical State." *Thyroid Research* 3, no. 11 (2010): doi:10.1186/1756-6614-3-11.

Tuso, Philip J., Mohamed H. Ismail, Benjamin P. Ha, and Carole Bartolotto. "Nutritional Update for Physicians: Plant-Based Diets." *The Permanente Journal* 17, no. 2 (Spring 2013): 61–66. doi:10.7812/TPP/12-085.

Vallath, Nandini. "Perspectives on Yoga Inputs in the Management of Chronic Pain." *Indian Journal of Palliative Care* 16, no. 1 (January–April 2010): 1–7. doi:10.4103/0973-1075.63127.

Vickers, A. J., A. M. Cronin, A. C. Maschino, G. Lewith, H. MacPherson, N. E. Foster, K. J. Sherman, et al. Acupuncture Trialists' Collaboration. "Acupuncture for Chronic Pain: Individual Patient Data Meta-Analysis." *Archives of Internal Medicine* 172, no. 19 (October 22 2012):1444–53. doi:10.1001/archinternmed.2012.3654.

Wilson, James. *Adrenal Fatigue: The 21st Century Syndrome.* Petaluma, CA: Smart Publications, 2001.

Wood, Rebecca. *The New Whole Foods Encyclopedia.* 2nd ed. New York: Penguin Group, 2010.

American College of Allergy, Asthma, and Immunology. "Types of Food Allergy: Milk and Dairy Allergy." Accessed July 28, 2015. www.acaai.org/allergies/types/food-allergies/types-food-allergy/milk-dairy-allergy.

American Heart Association. "Inflammation and Heart Disease." Accessed June 26, 2015. www.heart.org/HEARTORG/Conditions/Inflammation-and-Heart-Disease_UCM_432150_Article.jsp.

Center for Food Safety. "GE Food and Your Health." Accessed June 27, 2015. www.centerforfoodsafety.org/issues/311/ge-foods/ge-food-and-your-health#.

Centers for Disease Control and Prevention. "Allergies." Accessed June 25, 2015. www.cdc.gov/healthcommunication/ToolsTemplates/EntertainmentEd/Tips/Allergies.html.

Centers for Disease Control and Prevention. "Arthritis: National Statistics." Last updated February 25, 2015. Accessed June 25, 2015. www.cdc.gov/arthritis/data_statistics/national-statistics.html.

Centers for Disease Control and Prevention. "Epidemiology of the IBD." Last updated March 31, 2015. Accessed June 25, 2015. www.cdc.gov/ibd/ibd-epidemiology.htm.

Centers for Disease Control and Prevention. "FAQs about Hepatitis B Vaccine (Hep B) and Multiple Sclerosis." Last updated February 8, 2011. Accessed June 25, 2015. www.cdc.gov/vaccinesafety/Vaccines/multiplesclerosis_and_hep_b.html.

Centers for Disease Control and Prevention. "Heart Disease Facts." Accessed June 25, 2015. www.cdc.gov/heartdisease/facts.htm.

Centers for Disease Control and Prevention. "Number (in Millions) of Civilian, Noninstitutionalized Persons with Diagnosed Diabetes, United States, 1980–2011." Last updated March 28, 2013. Accessed June 25, 2015. www.cdc.gov/diabetes/statistics/prev/national/figpersons.htm.

Centers for Disease Control and Prevention. "Systemic Lupus Erythematosus." Last updated January 12, 2015. Accessed June 25, 2015. www.cdc.gov/arthritis/basics/lupus.htm.

CornAllergens.com. "Corn Allergen List." Accessed June 27, 2015. www.cornallergens.com/list/corn-allergen-list.php.

Crohn's and Colitis Canada. "Facts and Statistics." Accessed June 25, 2015. www.crohnsandcolitis.ca/site/c.dtJRL9NUJmL4H/b.9221471/k.5D6A/Facts_and_Statistics.htm.

Daniel, Kaayla. "Why Broth is Beautiful: Essential Roles for Proline, Glycine, and Gelatin." The Weston A. Price Foundation. June 18, 2003. Accessed June 29, 2015. www.westonaprice.org/health-topics/why-broth-is-beautiful-essential-roles-for-proline-glycine-and-gelatin/.

Encyclopedia Britannica. "Inflammation." Last updated April 11, 2014. Accessed June 24, 2015. www.britannica.com/science/inflammation.

Food Allergy Research & Education. "About Food Allergies: Milk Allergy." Accessed July 28, 2015. www.foodallergy.org/allergens/milk-allergy.

Food Allergy Research & Education. "About Food Allergies: Egg Allergy." Accessed July 28, 2015. www.foodallergy.org/allergens/egg-allergy.

GMO Compass. "USA 2013: No Reversal of Trend—Farmers Stick to Their Varieties of GM Crops." May 21, 2014. Accessed June 27, 2015. www.gmo-compass.org/eng/agri_biotechnology/gmo_planting/506.usa_cultivation_gm_plants_2013.html.

Harvard Health Publications: Harvard Medical School. "What You Eat Can Fuel or Cool Inflammation, a Key Driver of Heart Disease, Diabetes, and Other Chronic Conditions." Updated February 2007. Accessed June 24, 2015. www.health.harvard.edu/family_health_guide/what-you-eat-can-fuel-or-cool-inflammation-a-key-driver-of-heart-disease-diabetes-and-other-chronic-conditions.

Health Canada. "Food and Nutrition: Eggs—one of the top ten priority food allergens." Last modified September 26, 2012. Accessed July 28, 2015. www.hc-sc.gc.ca/fn-an/pubs/securit/2012-allergen_egg-oeuf/index-eng.php.

Hyman, Mark. "Inflammation: How to Cool the Fire Inside You That's Making You Fat and Diseased." Dr. Mark Hyman. January 27, 2012. Accessed June 24, 2015. www.drhyman.com/2012/01/27/inflammation-how-to-cool-the-fire-inside-you-thats-making-you-fat-and-diseased.

Hyman, Mark. "Is Your Body Burning Up With Hidden Inflammation?" *The Huffington Post*. September 24, 2009. Accessed June 24, 2015. www.huffingtonpost.com/dr-mark-hyman/is-your-body-burning-up-w_b_269717.html.

Institute for Agriculture and Trade Policy. "No Time to Lose: 147 Studies Supporting Public Health Action to Reduce Antibiotic Overuse in Food Animals." October 30, 2012. Accessed June 28, 2015. www.iatp.org/documents/no-time-to-lose.

Kresser, Chris. "Inflammation Worsens Danger of Heart Disease." Chris Kresser. January 22, 2009. Accessed June 26, 2015. www.chriskresser.com/inflammation-worsens-danger-of-heart-disease.

Lupus Foundation of America. "What Are the Common Symptoms of Lupus?" May 28, 2013. Accessed June 25, 2015. www.lupus.org/answers/entry/common-symptoms-of-lupus.

Lupus Foundation of America. "Statistics." Accessed July 28, 2015. www.lupus.org/about/statistics-on-lupus.

Medical News Today. "Inflammation: Causes, Symptoms and Treatment." Last updated May 25, 2015. Accessed June 24, 2015. www.medicalnewstoday.com/articles/248423.php.

Mercola, Joseph. "Bone Broth—One of Your Most Healing Diet Staples." Mercola.com. December 16, 2013. Accessed June 29, 2015. www.articles.mercola.com/sites/articles/archive/2013/12/16/bone-broth-benefits.aspx.

Mercola.com. "Why Grassfed Animal Products Are Better for You." Accessed June 28, 2015. www.mercola.com/beef/health_benefits.htm.

Migraine Research Foundation. "Migraine Fact Sheet." Accessed June 25, 2015. www.migraineresearchfoundation.org/fact-sheet.html.

National Foundation for Çeliac Awareness. "Celiac Disease Fast Facts." Last updated July 29, 2015. Accessed July 29, 2015. www.celiaccentral.org/celiac-disease/facts-and-figures.

National Heart, Lung, and Blood Institute. "What Is Asthma?" Accessed June 25, 2015. www.nhlbi.nih.gov/health/health-topics/topics/asthma.

National Institute on Alcohol Abuse and Alcoholism. "Beyond Hangovers: Understanding Alcohol's Impact on Your Health." September 2010. Accessed June 28, 2015. pubs.niaaa.nih.gov/publications/Hangovers/beyondHangovers.htm.

National Multiple Sclerosis Society. "Estimating the Prevalence of MS." Accessed June 25, 2015. www.nationalmssociety.org/About-the-Society/MS-Prevalence.

National Rosacea Society. "Rosacea Riddle Now Threatens More Than 16 Million Americans." April 1, 2010. Accessed June 25, 2015. www.rosacea.org/press/archive/20100401.php.

PubMed Health. "What Is an Inflammation?" Last updated January 2015. Accessed June 24, 2015. www.ncbi.nlm.nih.gov/pubmedhealth/PMH0072482.

Ravensthorpe, Michael. "Unhealthy Food Cravings Are a Sign of Mineral Deficiencies." NaturalNews.com. April 04, 2014 Accessed June 29, 2015. www.naturalnews.com/044579_food_cravings_mineral_deficiencies_essential_nutrients.html.

Romm, Cari. "The FDA Says Farmers Are Giving Animals Too Many Antibiotics." The Atlantic. October 3, 2014. www.theatlantic.com/health/archive/2014/10/american-meat-has-more-antibiotics-than-ever/381100.

Science Daily. "How Stress Influences Disease: Study Reveals Inflammation as the Culprit." April 12, 2012. Accessed June 24, 2015. www.sciencedaily.com/releases/2012/04/120402162546.htm.

University of Maryland Medical Center. "Omega-3 Fatty Acids." June 24, 2013. Accessed June 24, 2015. www.umm.edu/health/medical/altmed/supplement/omega3-fatty-acids.

U.S. Food and Drug Administration. "FDA Annual Summary Report on Antimicrobials Sold or Distributed in 2012 for Use in Food-Producing Animals." October 2, 2014. Accessed June 28, 2015. www.fda.gov/AnimalVeterinary/NewsEvents/CVMUpdates/ucm416974.htm.

U.S. National Library of Medicine: Medline Plus. "C-Reactive Protein." Updated February 11, 2013. Accessed June 24, 2015. www.nlm.nih.gov/medlineplus/ency/article/003356.htm.

Weil, Andrew. "Elevated C-Reactive Protein." Dr. Andrew Weil. Accessed June 25, 2015. www.drweil.com/drw/u/ART03424/Elevated-Creactive-Protein-CRP.html.

World Health Organization. "Headache Disorders." May 2012. Accessed June 25, 2015. www.who.int/mediacentre/factsheets/fs277/en.

World Health Organization. "Obesity and Overweight." Updated January 2015. Accessed June 25, 2015. www.who.int/mediacentre/factsheets/fs311/en.

World's Healthiest Foods. "Mediterranean Diet Reduces Inflammation." Accessed June 24, 2015. www.whfoods.org/genpage.php?tname=btnews&dbid=19.

World's Healthiest Foods. "What's New and Beneficial about Soybeans." Accessed June 27, 2015. www.whfoods.org/genpage.php?tname=foodspice&dbid=79.

World's Healthiest Foods. "What's New and Beneficial about Sweet Potatoes." Accessed June 28, 2015. www.whfoods.org/genpage.php?tname=foodspice&dbid=64.

Recipe Index

Index

CPSIA information can be obtained
at www.ICGtesting.com
Printed in the USA
BVHW06s1053180518
516527BV00001B/1/P

9 781641 522014